The
WISDOM of YOUR
SUBCONSCIOUS
MIND

by the same author

The
WISDOM of YOUR
SUBCONSCIOUS
MIND

John K. Williams

PRENTICE-HALL, INC.
Englewood Cliffs, New Jersey

Library of Congress Catalog Card Number:
64-14008

Printed in the United States of America
B&P 96150

Reward Edition . . . . . May, 1973

PRENTICE-HALL INTERNATIONAL, INC., *London*
PRENTICE-HALL OF AUSTRALIA, PTY., LTD., *Sydney*
PRENTICE-HALL OF CANADA, LTD., *Toronto*
PRENTICE-HALL FRANCE, S.A.R.L., *Paris*
PRENTICE-HALL OF INDIA (PRIVATE) LTD., *New Delhi*
PRENTICE-HALL OF JAPAN, INC., *Tokyo*

To My Granddaughter
LISA ANNE MOORE

Nov 3/44

Mind is the Master Power that moulds and makes
And Man is Mind, and evermore he takes
The Tool of thought, and shaping what he wills,
Brings forth a thousand joys, a thousand ills;
He thinks in secret and it comes to pass;
Environment is but his looking glass.

James Allen

CONTENTS

CONTENTS

PREFACE

THE data and the interpretations presented in this book have not emerged from structured, controlled experimentation.

Each human mind is unique, unlike any other mind. It follows that the processes of the human mind, its evaluation and response to any particular situation, are unique, disparate. There are, however, general trends, methods of stimulation and reaction, which appear as human behavior exhibits itself in the experience of living.

Observation and investigation indicate that the human mind or personality functions through a two-fold unitary process. The concept generally accepted among scientific investigators and the conclusions arising from observation is that the structure of personality or mind consists of a conscious or volitional activity designed primarily to assure survival in practical experience and a deep strata of subconscious energy, which is the source of creative insight and of the emerging synthesis of mental processes, ordinarily called intuition and inspiration.

It is the purpose of this empirical study to interpret for the average person the function of the self-aware aspect of mind and its control of the underlying area of creative energy which together make possible self-directed achievement.

The material presented and the techniques described will be of assistance to those engaged in basic and applied research, to professional and educational personnel, to executives who must direct and guide employees, to those interested in interpersonal and public relations, to parents facing the problem of creating wholesome family life and to men and women in all walks of life who hope to stabilize and control their mental and emotional processes and thereby gain a greater degree of peace of mind and personal satisfaction in the day-to-day experience of living.

In the field of psychology and in the interpretation of mental and emotional activity, as observed in the experience exhibited by the average person, originality is difficult, if not impossible, to achieve. During several years of observation and study it is quite possible that concepts and ideas described and expressed by other writers have unintentionally been used without credit to the original source. If this has occurred, I express to all involved my deep regret and sincere apology. To the authors and publishers who have granted permission to use quotations from their copyrighted work, I also express a full measure of gratitude for their courtesy.

John K. Williams

Birmingham, Alabama

PROLOGUE

OUR forms of legal and social control, as well as the validity of our ethical concepts are based upon the assumption that the individual has a built-in endowment of volitional strength and understanding by which he can determine and control his activity. This idea of individual responsibility and self-direction is embodied in every culture and social group—whether advanced or primitive. True or false, this assumption that the behavior of a person is selected and determined by that person himself depends upon the nature and structure of personality—the capability of the mind of the individual to achieve and maintain self-direction.

Throughout this book I have assumed explicitly the dictum of Cudworth that "Mind is senior to the world and the architect thereof." The creative insight and wisdom of the subconscious mind when properly understood and correctly applied, sustain the following four statements:

First, you are the architect of your destiny. Every experience or condition in your life—poverty or riches, success or failure, health or illness—is the result of action and purpose set in motion by you.

Second, within the area of your life, you have creative power.

You can make a mental image or blueprint of the progress and expansion you want to achieve, and by impressing the concept of your objective upon your subconscious mind, you can cause the condition you visualize in your mind to be created. Creative energy is the self-induced action of mind upon itself and within itself. The force behind all progress and achievement is energy created and applied by mind.

Third, you are a radiating power. By expanding your consciousness, you can attract what you want. Like the lowly amoeba, you can have only what you can surround and absorb within yourself. The Universe cannot and does not give you anything. It does give you, however, the power and challenge to achieve, to create for yourself the conditions and resources you want. You can have anything you want, provided you are willing to pay the price.

Fourth, you are the building and directing power of your life. Life develops only by mental and emotional power from within. Centuries ago, Hermes, one of the greatest teachers and philosophers of all times, made the statement, "All is Mind." Mental and emotional processes create and control all that comes into your experience. Nothing has ever been, is now or ever will be, that is not the result of mind action. Since this law is universal and inescapable, it follows that man in his nature and aspirations is not obsolete; that man has essential freedom of action in determining the content of his experience; and that mind, or personality, is more and something other than the ephemeral reactions of biochemical processes in the brain.

Notwithstanding this basic concept, understood for centuries, it is a matter of everyday observation that the great majority of people live lives of quiet desperation and frustration. Too many people inhabit the haunted hinterlands of failure, anxiety and illness. This is frequently true whether or not the person has achieved financial competency or status in the community.

Consider the achievements of our affluent social order, made possible by scientific industrial technology: We have the most abundant, immediately available food supply ever provided any people. Our medical and sanitary measures guard health and life to a greater extent than has been true in any other culture, past or present. Through our Social Security program and other retirement systems, the aging population is sustained to a degree unique in human history. We have the most expensive and efficient educational system ever projected. Our democratic form of government and our courts safeguard the individual more completely than during the days of glory in Athens. The average person enjoys luxuries and conveniences unequaled by the citizens of any other nation or in any previous age. Despite all of this, we are frustrated, phobia-ridden and without meaningful motivation as to the content and purpose of life.

As a result of our mental and emotional imbalance, we have a crime rate which at times threatens the stability of our social and legal processes. Delinquency, divorce and broken homes and chronic alcoholism constitute immediate problems for which the behavioral sciences and the medical profession are unable to offer even a partial solution.

We have achieved so little self-direction and created such meager inner resources that millions of people turn to chemical agents to control and stimulate their emotions. The enormous sales of the so-called tranquilizing and psychic energizing drugs is a disturbing symptom which reveals the paucity of our inner poise and motivation for creative achievement. The crescendo of the excessive consumption of alcohol is another effort to quiet our frustrated emotions and to compensate for our feeling of sterile immaturity.

To an extent seldom realized, we are "brain-washed" by our ubiquitous mass communication media. To escape from ourselves, we feed our emotions the drama of horror and stark realism and more recently we are entertained by the bizarre and perhaps informing scenes and reactions to be found only in the treatment room of a psychiatric physician. The literature of crime, perversion, violence and abnormal sexuality implants a pattern of thinking which limits and frequently destroys creative ability. Since the average person does not understand that our lives are controlled by emotional forces, the trauma produced by such mental and emotional nutrients, although the process is not consciously observed, is compounded many times.

About two years ago one of the leading intellectual magazines of the nation carried an article titled "The Americanization of the Unconscious." * The writer of this article, a psychiatric physician, recognizes the growing concept among professional social workers, counselors and some members of the legal profession, as well as among the general population, that the unconscious mind (more correctly described as the subconscious mind) is a built-in source of energy, complex or mechanism which cannot be controlled by the individual—that the individual is helpless in the presence of these inner forces which motivate his behavior.

Perhaps no great thinker has been more misunderstood than Sigmund Freud. True, his concepts are being modified and changed by many authorities, but it was certainly not his basic intention to teach that the individual is the helpless victim of instinctual drives and forces built into his personality. Whatever the cause, the last quarter century has witnessed an increasing acceptance of the idea that the individual, due largely to traumatic experiences in childhood, is unable to achieve and sustain self-direction. Interestingly enough, during this same period it has been amply demonstrated that the individual is always in command of himself, that in any situation he does what at the time he wants to do.

It is, of course, true that the failure to direct, and to understand the creative insight, energy and wisdom of the subconscious mind, brings many people to the point of no return—a dominating, controlling pattern of mental activity has been established, which is irreversible. The point to be remembered is that there was a time in the life of the individual when by proper direction this process in his life could have been directed and channeled into constructive and creative work.

Due to the prevailing self-limiting currents in our present intellectual and moral climate, we are to a significant degree adopting

* Dr. John R. Seeley in *Atlantic*, Vol. 208 No. 1, p. 68.

a philosophy of "escapism" rather than developing the concept of individual and social responsibility, based upon the self-directing capability of the human personality.

In this book I have attempted to outline a sound philosophy of the human mind as the creative source of every experience in the life of the individual. Techniques and methods have been described by which the creative insight and the wisdom of the subconscious mind may be found and used in building the individual life to it's highest potential. This concept of the mind and the techniques suggested are not theoretical in nature but are supported by the experience of men and women in every culture and in every walk of life. The considerations advanced in this book account not only for the experience of success and satisfaction but also for failure and frustration. For the solution of problems inherent in human experience, no miracle-working formula or program is available. The response of the individual is the cause of success or failure.

The human mind (in its unitary action as conscious and subconscious) despite all its distortions and limitations is an expression of the highest wisdom of the Universe. It is through the self-aware action of mind that beauty, truth and goodness are known and success and peace of mind achieved.

1
THE CHALLENGE
OF THE
PRESENT SITUATION

THE earth on which we live is one of nine planets of a rather mediocre sun, around which all are revolving and at the same time continually spinning on their axes. Our sun around which these nine planets are moving belongs to a galaxy made up of 100 billion other suns; the nearest of these suns is four and one third light years away and the most distant 100,000 or more light years. A light year, as everyone knows, is the distance light travels in a year at the rate of 186,000 miles a second.

This island Universe to which the nine planets and our sun belongs is about 100,000 light years in diameter and viewed from a remote point in space would appear to be a spiral nebula, much like the pictures of spiral nebulae to be seen at any planetarium.

The known immensity of the Cosmos is inconceivable. Beyond our galaxy of stars there are several billion other island universes, each containing billions of suns. The nearest to our own galaxy being about 150,000,000 light years distant. The most distant is perhaps ten billion light years away. Modern astronomy can locate a billion or more galaxies, each containing billions of flaming suns. Sir James Jeans has written, "The number of stars in the Universe is practically like the number of grains of sand on all the seashores of the world." Each star on the average is a billion times the volume of the earth and yet so vast is the Cosmos that there are millions and millions of miles between each of them.

Turning from the magnitude of the Cosmos to the minute, consider an infinitely small particle of matter. This particle of matter is barely visible, yet it contains millions and millions of molecules. A molecule consists of two or more atoms and an atom has one or more electrons revolving around a nucleus of one or more protons. These billions of stars, our sun, the earth and all material bodies as well as the atoms of which they are composed, are all made of the same thing—something which we cannot see and which we cannot locate by touch. Science describes this basic element as energy. It is known that atoms are miniature solar systems with electrons spinning at tremendous speeds around a nucleus of protons. It is also known that electrons and protons and other subatomic elements are simply units of negative and positive electrical energy.

The Cosmos, every material thing in it, is made of energy. There is enough energy concentrated in a small lump of coal to drive a large steamship across the Atlantic and back; in the atoms of a cup of water there is enough energy to light a large city for a year. This energy of the Cosmos has a vast variety of forms, the bottled-up being called "matter" and the unbottled, "radiation."

According to the equation worked out by Einstein, and now regarded as the foundation of theoretical physics and modern technology, every gram of matter (of any kind) has stored within it the equivalent of 25,000,000 kilowatt hours of energy.

Cosmic energies are streams of electrons—not matter, but radiation. All matter is composed of radiation. The source of cosmic energy is outside the confines of the physical Universe. Certainly there was no energy in the physical Universe previous to its creation.

Now visualize the Cosmos as far as one can conceive of it. It is of a magnitude that is overwhelming and of subatomic minuteness that is utterly inconceivable. All the parts are made of the same thing. They are all in unceasing activity and all activities are so ordered that they form an organic whole.

The physicist Heisenberg observes that the Cosmos is composed of unitary energy, and the outlook of the "new physics" tends to the concept that the Cosmos as we know it is composed of, or derived from, one all-inclusive force or energy. This idea of the unity of the Cosmos is not new. It is as old as thinking man, and actually is the scientific basis of the Hindu conception of the divine Vishnu as the all-pervading sustainer of the Cosmos. It does not matter what word is used—whether "life" or "energy"—the fact remains that there is essentially only one source and sustaining basis of everything in the Cosmos regardless of the varied forms in which the products of that unitary energy or force may be exhibited.

Matter is now best visualized as almost empty space. The atom itself has all but vanished into a series of electric charges, waves and probabilities, no longer understandable except in terms of mathematical equations. The Cosmos is exploding and moving with terrific speed across infinite distance. Space is curved. Light waves can be bent, and form and mass depend upon speed of motion.

The mystery and the vastness of the Cosmos as revealed by the discoveries of modern astronomy, as well as by the new insights of theoretical physics, tend to obscure the potential dynamics of the human mind. The physical world of yesteryear with all its compact and assuring structure is gone forever.

The mental and emotional processes and values held by individuals and groups develop gradually over long periods of time. This accounts for the resistance always offered when new insights and discoveries regarding the nature and destiny of man seem to threaten long-held thought patterns. This opposition is frequently, if not always, expressed regardless of the value or correctness of the new concepts.

During recent centuries the ideas which man holds regarding the Universe and himself have been challenged in three major areas of investigation. Previous to the time of Copernicus humanity regarded the earth as the center of the Universe. The earth was believed to be the only area on which the life process exhibited itself. Beginning with the thinking of Copernicus and expanded by the explorations of astronomy it is now known that the earth is but a second-rate planet, revolving around a third-class sun and is, in fact, only one of millions of other planetary units in the depth of space. This insight removed this planet from its central point in Cosmos and reduced its position to one of little, if any, significance in the whole Scheme of Things.

With the Darwinian statement of the theory of evolution and its wide acceptance, especially in the scientific world, human dignity suffered another blow. Man is no longer a unique creation with an immortal soul, embodying moral and ethical elements of transcendent value. Human life and experience are the result of a long process by natural forces without known purpose and without previous design as to the ultimate goal. Man shares his heritage and development with the complex animal life from the amoeba to the organism known as Homo sapiens. The mental and emotional processes found in human personality are the result of the configuration of atomic particles knocking themselves about within the area of the human brain. Mental activity is resident in and emerges from matter.

Following almost immediately upon the Darwinian theory came the Freudian concept. Man no longer controls his own life. He is but the helpless pawn of unconscious forces and energies which determine his behavior and limit his achievement. The ideas enunciated by Freud, and further developed by mechanistic psychology, have so permeated man's thinking about himself that he no longer believes that he is capable of self-control, and this means that moral and ethical standards have little, if any meaning. Man's life is controlled not by processes which he sets in motion within himself but is the result of unconscious instincts and drives built into his personality. These forces are below the level of consciousness. The individual is, therefore, to a large degree without responsibility for his behavior. Since the ideas of Freud resulted from his study of pathology, little, if any, recognition was given to the impact which environmental factors of a constructive nature make upon the individual. Freud also failed to consider (certainly not adequately) the integrative and creative instinctual energy and drive which are unquestionably present in the submerged area of personality.

Thus modern man, with his residence demoted from a central place in Cosmos to a position of vast insignificance, sharing his heritage with the animal kingdom, and rendered further helpless by the unconscious instincts and drives within his own life, has experienced traumatic insults to his dignity and status which result in anxiety, frustration and the loss of self-direction.

Our present day utility-minded culture is face to face with the threat of complete destruction by nuclear weapons. This fact with all its potential for humanity exists in the same social order with another equally grave situation. Advancing knowledge has placed instruments more deadly than those of atomic power into the grasp of whatever individual or group that attains control of political power. Techniques now exist (and are being applied in some parts of the world) not only for mass destruction, but also for controlling and warping the minds of men.

The development of these instruments of physical destruction and the methods of mass mental and emotional control are only in their infancy, and what the end of this will be no one can foretell. The future is an enigma in which only one thing stands out clearly: It is fraught with terrific and accelerating danger.

Notwithstanding the obviously immediate threat of physical destruction and the equally present danger of psychological domination by political power, it is necessary to remind ourselves that the intellectual climate of this period has little interest in the ultimate meaning and destiny of life presently exhibiting on this planet.

The search for truth has lost its challenge. Too many suffer from intellectual and spiritual fatigue. We have a passion for things, for bodily comforts and mental sedatives. This generation suffers from *ennui* and a lack of goal-directed purposes. It naturally follows from this intellectual and social situation that we have little interest in and, therefore, give little time to exploring the vast uncharted land within the human mind.

Man has created instruments that measure space 100,000,000

light-years deep. He surveys the internal structure of the atom and taps its power. Man does not explore, and fails to recognize the extent of the creative power within his own mind. Indeed, man is a mystery to himself, a mystery which remains unsolved even when death's bitter waters begin to rise about him.

The prophetic statement of that tough-minded Britisher, Winston Churchill, is of current significance: "Without an equal growth of Mercy, Pity, Peace and Love, science herself may destroy all that makes human life majestic and tolerable." The trouble comes when men of science leave their laboratories and become philosophers. The purpose of life, the value of individual and social experience, the destiny of the human personality cannot be measured by a slide rule, nor can they be found on an agar plate or in a test tube. They will be found, if found at all, in the *origin* and *nature* of *personality* and in the unrecognized and little-known *borderland areas* of the mind itself.

To deal adequately with the challenge of the present situation some generally held current assumptions must be reexamined and evaluated. This rethinking and evaluating process will, if the true scientific ideal is held in mind, lead to the significant conclusion that the complex mental and emotional processes observed in human life are an expression of mind energy resident in the human personality.

Mind has its roots in, and emerges from, a field of reality which transcends our space-time continuum. Mind is the measuring rod of reality and is limited in its action and expression only by the nature of its own being. While this insight has an obscure place in our present day intellectual climate, it is not new. It is found at the center of every great religious tradition. It is the great Intuition grounded deep in the structure of personality. It follows, because of its inherent nature, that the human mind is greater than we ordinarily believe . . . that it has powers seldom recognized and that it functions in a borderland area greater in extent and significance than that revealed by our everyday self-aware experience.

2
THE PRIMACY
OF MIND

NOTWITHSTANDING our technological progress, shadows cross the pathway of future achievement. The danger resulting from atomic power and our lack of capacity to make constructive use of it is growing every day. We are in the midst of a revolution in our physical environment so vast and so utterly beyond anything we have experienced in the past that the human mind is uncertain of the outcome. We have one foot in a civilization that died over Nagasaki and Hiroshima and another foot in a world civilization that is struggling to be born. Yet, the unconquerable urge in the mind of man to explore, to seek knowledge about himself, his environment, and the forces by which he is surrounded, will continue. It is the noblest expression of the human mind, giving life its value and purpose, clothing it with dignity.

Humanity is not being destroyed by science. The betrayal, if it comes, will be by men without social and spiritual insight. The long road toward goals of social organization and moral idealism, now but dimly seen, will emerge clear and distinct. Over these roads humanity will move to a more satisfying way of life.

Extended though the range of modern science may be, this area of knowledge represents, as its most cogently thinking prophets are the first to admit, only a narrow glance and perhaps an incorrect view of the unknown and infinite realm of reality as exhibited by laws and processes which we can observe.

To build a philosophy and social outlook that will permit the full expression of the human potential, we must have a frame of reference, a starting point. A foundation must be constructed (or assumed) on which the creative power of mind and personality can operate. For this foundation to be adequate it must be grounded in the very nature of the cosmic process. Consider then the two current hypotheses which attempt to account for the creation and structure of the Cosmos, including, of necessity, the mind of man.

During recent years evidence has been accumulating that the distant galaxies of stars and suns apparently are moving away from the earth, and the speed of their recession increases with their distance. It is as though there were some kind of explosion going on with its center in our galaxy, and everything else in the Universe moving outward away from us. The outward speed of a galaxy is about 100 miles per second for each million light-years. If this velocity were maintained for some millions of years, which is a short time in the earth's history, the star bodies we now observe will have disappeared beyond the "horizon" of the observable Universe.

This phenomena has given rise to the term, "expansion of the Universe" or "movement toward infinity." Several theories have been advanced. *In the theory of continuous creation* put forward by the British astronomer Hoyle, new nebulae are formed by the energy of the Cosmos, replacing those galaxies that disappear beyond the horizon.

Another theory has been advanced which involves the assumption of an *explosive creation*. According to this theory, all the matter in the entire Universe came into existence during an explosion of neutrons, which lasted only about five minutes. As the result of this original eruption, all the stars and galaxies were formed. The impact of this tremendous explosion is the cause of the outward motion of the galaxies. The theory assumes that this explosive creation occurred about six billion years ago.

The inquiring mind must ask who or what set in motion this outrush of energy and creative force at a rate and on a scale that staggers our imagination. Was it a planned action? Did it embody within itself the plan of an orderly Universe and the evolution of life? What mind, energy or force created the explosive neutrons? Did the neutrons hold a conference, decide to pool their resources, and thus bring the omniverse into being? Is it reasonable to assume the absence of a *planner* when the *plan* is evident? Did Infinite Mind preside at the birth of the Universe? Why violate the basic assumption of the human mind: *Ex nihilo nihil fit* (From nothing, nothing comes). Must we suppose that a ship might be constructed of such kind that entirely by itself it could sail from place to place for years without end, adjusting itself to varying winds, avoiding shoals, casting and weighing anchor, seeking safe harbor when necessary and doing all that a normal ship might do? This without Captain or Navigator?

Pain and pleasure, loss and frustration, along with achievement seem to be an inherent ingredient in the cosmic process. And whether this is a mistake in the design, or part of the design is a question that sooner or later must spring to the mind of every thoughtful person.

A few billion years past, the planet on which we live was hot gas, thrown off from the sun by some cosmic accident. During long eons of time it cooled and in the primordial sea minute forms of life appeared. The story is now familiar to every school child—the spread of plant life to the barren shores, the invasion of land and air by animals from the sea, the struggle to survive, the failure and triumphs, finally man himself, the highest but not necessarily the completion of this long process of evolution.

Regardless of the development achieved by Homo sapiens, there must once more come a time when the earth will be unable to support life. The sun will die out like an exhausted lamp. Even the stars are not immortal.

The general verdict of science is that the entire Cosmos is under a death sentence. It will continue infinitely longer than living creatures, but it will not last forever. It had a beginning and it will have an end. After untold eons of time all the creative energy of the Universe will reach a dead equilibrium.

In building a philosophy that will permit and sustain creative achievement we cannot help asking whether there is a purpose behind this apparently meaningless activity. What is man's place in this utterly mysterious Universe? Is human life—life of any kind—no more than a chance product of mingling molecules millions of years ago? In cold despair must we accept the assumption of Lord Russell, "Man is the product of causes which had no prevision of the end they were achieving: his origin, his growth, his hopes and fears, his loves and beliefs are but the outcome of accidental collocations of atoms."

In a challenging phrase, T. S. Eliot once described atheism as "a well-lighted road in a desert." He meant that this is all a purely materialistic science can show us—a highly efficient system of illumination and a well-made road leading nowhere. Human life came from nothing and soon shall become nothing again. To the materialist, life is no more than a "useless passion," a bubble bursting in the air.

On the other hand, is there some pattern which our intellects may dimly comprehend—some distant vista of purpose and values, evidence of a Design and a Designer.

From all the data available it appears necessary to assume that some Inscrutable Mind or Consciousness is evidently at work in the process and arrangement of cells in living organisms, as well as in the march through space of worlds and stars.

Coming from the mind of an eminent scientist, perhaps the statement of Dr. Robert A. Millikan has evidential value: "We have come from somewhere and we are going somewhere. The Great Architect of the Universe never built a stairway that leads to nowhere." From another discipline of science, that of biology, Dr. Edward Sinnott of Yale supports the assumption that "purpose is inherent in the life process."

If the objective of the cosmic process is purposeful, involving design or plan, then this assumption makes necessary and evident a Planner or Designer. Purposeful planning is the result of mind activity. No blueprint for the construction of a building has ever been made except by the mind of an architect. Mental and social stability, sanity, creative insight and activity depend upon the concept that an Inscrutable Mind is the basis and ground of the potentiality of the life process as it exhibits itself on this planet. This assumption was cogently stated by Plotinus centuries ago: "The most irrational theory of all is that elements without intelligence should produce intelligence."

Certainly man's mind stands at the apex of the evolutionary process. "All our dignity exists in thought," said Pascal. "On earth there is nothing great but man; in man there is nothing great but mind," wrote Sir William Hamilton. Epictetus went even further and described reason as "a fragment of God." The higher the estimate our own age makes of man's mental power the better, for every aspect of reality is understood and evaluated by mental processes within man himself.

To understand man's ability to control his mind and direct it into creative channels, one must arrive at a correct viewpoint regarding the relation of mental activity to the human brain. The brain is the instrument of mind—mind is therefore not the product of chemical activity within this organ. A useful concept is that ideas exist as energies in the Cosmos and the human mind acts as a receiver and transmitter. Thus thoughts are picked or selected and sent to different levels of consciousness, their directional flow and voltage more often than not determined subconsciously. In line with Bergson's concept, mental energies pour through the brain to be sifted, adapted or directed, depending upon the interest and purpose of the individual mind. Being only an instrument, the physical brain is limited to receiving and holding only those thoughts which tend to assure survival. Between brain and mind as much difference exists as between a switchboard and a person originating or receiving the message that goes through it.

Consider the notion widely held that every idea a man has ever had and every sensation he has ever experienced leaves an indelible imprint on the substance of the brain. Investigation and research in psychology and physiology, implemented by all the precision instruments of modern science, have failed to find a single datum to support this idea. "The brain does not secrete thought as the liver secretes bile. The mind is not in the brain, nor, in fact, is the mind anywhere in the universe of space . . ."[1]

Thinking, mental activity, is not the result of processes *originated* by the brain. Memories are not "stored" in the brain. In point of fact, there is no anatomical evidence that man has a mind. No marks or imprints are found in or on the brain, or in or on any tissue or structure of the body, as the result of a lifetime of mental activity. "The realms of mind are not confined within man's skull."

Thinking is not done by the brain, it is accomplished by mind, or consciousness. Mind is certainly not identical with brain activity; it belongs to a totally different category of reality.

Samuel Roth in his book, *The Peep Hole of the Universe*, says that "Consciousness is the ultimate unit of which all matter is spun." We must, therefore, assume that consciousness is a thing-in-itself. Regardless of where you look, you are looking into your mind. Matter as such is not *what* you see but the *way* in which you are seeing reality. Consciousness is the ultimate substance of the Universe. It operates and creates, with our bodies as focal points of immanentism.

Professor A. S. Eddington writing as a mathematical physicist in 1920 said that "all through the physical world runs that unknown content which must be the stuff of our consciousness."

"Amid all the mysteries by which we are surrounded," wrote Herbert Spencer, "nothing is more certain than that we are ever in the presence of an infinite and eternal energy from which all things proceed."

The highest expression of consciousness is through and by the instrument we know as personality—the word "personality" is used here to indicate the entire synthesis which makes up the individual human being. The biologist H. J. Haldane once wrote, "Personality is the great central fact of the Universe." The spectrum of being

---

[1] Boris Sidis, M.D., *The Psychology of Suggestion* (New York: Appleton-Century-Crofts). Used by permission.

extends beyond the boundary of what we ordinarily believe to be our total selves.

One of the great thinkers of this period, Sir Arthur Eddington, has said that "Mind is the first and most direct thing in our experience, all else is remote inference." Is it reasonable to assume that consciousness—

> The eye with which the Universe
> Beholds itself and knows itself—

is simply a thing among other things to be placed alongside the river or the stone?

In another connection Eddington expresses his conviction that "The mind has the power to affect groups of atoms and even tamper with the odds of atomic behavior, and that even the course of the world is not predetermined by physical laws but may be altered by the uncaused volition of human beings."

The basic question is, can mind illumine its own path, select the direction in which it will go, or is man a helpless puppet in the hands of his own body? It is to mind, or consciousness, that we must look for the key to life's meaning. As Milton said, "The mind is its own place and in itself can make a heaven of hell—a hell of heaven."

There is a passage in *Bhagavad-Gita* (The Song of the Blessed) which reads, "Man is made by his belief. As he believes, so he is."

In an attempt to evaluate the creative power and energy of mind it must be remembered that this evaluation and all criticism of the mind is done by the mind itself.

The uncounted millions of worlds, each moving according to plan within the limitless expanse of the Universe, are composed of energy. And energy is but the self-induced action of mind upon itself and within itself. *Mind is all there is in the Universe.* It is Mind that creates *time, space, motion,* and the *reality of matter.* Material substances, regardless of *solidity, density* or *size,* are but the result of mind action. This is not to deny the *reality* of *matter.* On the contrary, it gives to so-called matter undying reality. The impression of a normal mind is that the foundation structure of matter *is energy applied by mind.*

The ancient Hermetic insight states a profound truth: As it is above, so it is below. Life or mind functions on all levels of reality in keeping with its own nature. Mind responds to mind. Energy follows the action of mind. The responses of Ultimate Mind to individual mind is determined by the concept of its nature and function projected by the action of the individual mind. The response of Ultimate Mind is as the individual mind conceives of that response.

Consciousness, the creative source or ground of all reality, is single, not plural. It is a unitary process and functions as such. The unitary process expresses itself in all the varied forms and conditions observed by self-aware individual units of mind. These multiphasic exhibitions of reality are to the individual mind as the mind of the individual sees them. The observer sees reality through the lens of his own mental and emotional apparatus. In a very real sense the observer and the object of his evaluation are one and the same thing. It is this identity of the observer and the thing observed which permits the creative power of mind to function.

From these considerations of the primacy of mind, two facts stand out. The first fact: Mind is the ultimate reality in the Universe. The world of things, of material forms which we see and touch is the result of creative power inherent in mind. Whatever is formed by mind can be unformed by mind. Since mind is the only creative originating source, nothing other than mind can come into existence.

The second fact: You are mind. A person does not have a mind. *A person is mind.* All that a person is—including the conditions of success or failure which surround the individual—is the result of mind action. Given adequate understanding of its nature and function, mind will make available to you whatever you need for growth and enhancement.

The basic assumption of this study is that within the human mind and out beyond the presently recognized limits of its activity there is a world of values, of creative power, of meaningful relationships; a field of beauty and harmony of which we are only dimly aware, and which we have explored all too little. If this second assumption is true, then we can build a new faith in the Universe, "a faith that will take the place of the vast sense of fear, frustration and futility that, like a shadow, darkens the goal of all human effort."

Certainly the evidence points toward the existence of an area of human personality lying behind and beyond conscious awareness and which, except in rare moments, is hidden from view. Strange things evidently happen in this region, but not things without order and purpose. They are correlated both with another and with normal experience. They are not "white elephants"—scandalous interlopers into law and order which it is bad scientific taste to consider. Such phenomena, indeed, introduces us into a strange realm. We may picture it in our minds as a newly discovered hall in the mansion of nature; not an imaginary fairlyland, peopled by fantasy and illusion.

3

THE NATURE OF THE MIND—SELF-DIRECTING AND CREATIVE

RECENTLY the president of one of the largest aerospace companies of the nation spoke to a joint session of the legislature of Alabama. This man directs the work of 80,000 employees located at several points throughout the nation. Of this group of 80,000 employees, one of each four is a highly trained engineer. He was invited to address the legislature in recognition of his achievement and leadership in the field of aerospace planning and manufacturing.

This man was born in Walker County, Alabama, and during the period of his youth, this section was devoted almost exclusively to coal mining. He himself was born and reared in a barren, isolated coal mining community. During his early adult years he worked in one of these mines digging coal. Notwithstanding his present position of leadership, he still retains his last suit of mining clothes and the small lamp which he, as a miner, wore on his cap to furnish light for his work.

How does one account for this man's success and for the barren, poverty-stricken lives still being experienced by so many of those with whom he had early association? It is logical to assume that he had some special intellectual endowment, or that he had connections with influential people which gave him his opportunity.

Neither condition is true. Was it luck or some special circumstance which provided him with this opportunity for leadership? In fact, he enjoyed no special privilege and no opportunity not open to anyone in Walker County or anywhere else.

This man's attainment and leadership is in no way unique. For some unknown reason a few individuals obtain positions of responsibility and leadership, while the great masses of people live out their lives in failure and frustration. This man, along with thousands of others in American industry and business, has tapped a source of power not recognized or used by the average man.

A Chinese in the early days of San Francisco stood spellbound at the sight of a cable car. "No pushee. No pullee. Go allee samee like hellee!" Unlike this migrant from the hinterland of ancient Cathay, the president of this aerospace company identified and put into use the largely unrecognized creative power of mind.

It is, of course, not possible to understand the ultimate nature of mind. It is, however, possible to observe the way mind functions, how it creates and how it achieves its objective; and from this knowledge to be able to control the activity of mind and direct it toward the accomplishment of any purpose we desire to achieve.

Since the essential nature of mind cannot be fully know until the origin and nature of the Cosmic Process is known, we must proceed on the assumption that mind is and that we can observe its activities within our own personality and in other persons.

There is one basic fact observed by all investigators. Mind functions on two levels, or in two areas, namely, the conscious, self-aware part of mind and the creative subconscious level. This two-fold nature of mind activity does not indicate two minds or one mind with two separate divisions. Mind is a unity and functions as such. The two-fold activity of mind is an interrelated process.

Psychologists have used various illustrative analogies to describe the relationship and function of two levels of mind. One approach to this problem is by comparing the conscious and subconscious mind to coral islands found in some parts of the ocean. On the surface of these coral islands there is a small circular ridge of a rock-like substance surrounded by ocean water. On this protruding ledge is found a fringe of tropic vegetation. This is all there is to be seen on the surface, with no suggestion of the mighty structure down to the ocean's floor built by uncountable millions of coral creatures during eons of time. The human mind is to a degree like these coral islands.

By far the largest area of mind is built up with associated sense impressions and memories of all past experiences. This submerged area of mentation is the creative part of mind. The conscious mind corresponds to the tropic vegetation resting on and deriving its power from the massive structure found below the level of the water. In the conscious mind there are certain perceptions, emotions, impulses and ideas selected and set in motion by itself. This mental and emotional activity is reflected in the sunlight of self-awareness.

One authority in this field described the human mind as being similar to an old-fashioned well six or eight feet in diameter, walled up with stones and filled with water. This well is the human mind. He thinks of this well of water as being connected with and a part of an infinite ocean of water. From the subterranean depth of the great ocean of life, mental activity moves up through that well into the experience of the individual. The only point at which the infinite reservoir of mind activity can be observed is at the very surface of the well.

This writer thinks of the surface of the well as the conscious mind, the area of self-aware experience. Just below the conscious level, or surface of the mind, is that area of mental and emotional activity usually described as the subconscious mind. This subconscious mind carries with it all the mental images and emotional states which have been experienced during the life of the individual. The subconscious level of mind contacts a volume of experience and reality much greater in extent and in creative power than the conscious part of the mind.[1]

A significant analogy is found by comparing the subconscious and the conscious regions of mind to the visible and invisible areas

[1] Dan Custer, *The Miracle of Mindpower* (Englewood Cliffs, N.J.: Prentice-Hall, Inc.). Used by permission.

of the spectrum of light. It is known that the visible portion of the light spectrum with its red, orange, green, blue, indigo and violet rays is bounded on one end by a region of infrared rays and on the other end by ultraviolet rays. These invisible fields of light extend indefinitely in either direction. These hidden rays are invisible to normal eyes but are recorded by scientific instruments. The larger part of the heat rays of the light spectrum is invisible to us and forms a part of the infrared area of the light spectrum. In a similar manner, the major portion of the chemical changes in the plant world results from the action of the ultraviolet rays which are invisible to the unaided eyes of the individual. In the light spectrum there are x-rays and y-rays, all differing from light only in respect of their wavelengths. There are alpha rays, which radium discharges with the velocity of 10,000 miles a second, and there are the recently discovered cosmic rays, of penetrating power 200 times greater than any of the rest, and more powerful by day than by night, whose source no one knows.

Considering this analogy, the first fact to be noted is that the part of the light spectrum visible to our sight, without instruments, is very small. In terms of extent, perhaps not one-thousandth part of the total spectrum of light can be observed by normal human eyes. This fact corresponds to the range of the conscious mind. We know that of the total personality the conscious mind is a limited section of a range of reality which extends indefinitely beyond the self-aware aspect of mind.

The second fact to be noted is that portions of the light spectrum beyond the visible part can in some degree be observed by instruments and to a still greater degree the presence of these invisible light rays can be known by the results they produce. In a somewhat similar way we know something of the work of the subconscious by the insights and intuitions which emerge from it into the conscious area of mind. In many aspects of nature, and especially in the physiologic processes of the human body, we can observe what seems to be infinite wisdom at work in sustaining those obscure processes by which life is exhibited in our world of time and space.

In the spectrum of light there are areas almost totally unknown to the human mind but which certainly exist. Cosmic rays are an example. In the field of extrasensory perception, particularly the areas described as telepathy and intuition, there are activities and processes observed under certain conditions but of which we have no explanation except that these activities emerge from a vast subconscious area of mind.

While no analogy is perfect and can be pressed too far, it is certainly true that the conscious mind is a very limited part of our personality and that there are areas of reality and mentation which extend beyond the area of mental and emotional activity which we ordinarily believe to be total self, or personality.

For another approach, we may compare the conscious and subconscious areas of mentation to a small, luminous circle surrounded by extended circles of twilight and beyond this an indefinite area of darkness. The events occurring in the twilight zone and in the extended region of darkness are quite as real as those occurring within the limited area of the luminous circle.

All competent investigators now assume that the conscious part of the mind is a very limited and restricted area of the total personality. This conscious part of the mind extends in varying degrees out into an infinitely larger area of reality. This extension of the conscious mind is through the subconscious areas in the twilight zone of our analogy.

Again, we may compare the mind to the planet on which we live, with its underlying deposits of coal and oil, its infinite power of electromagnetic energy. In these hidden sources is potential power awaiting some appropriate stimulus to bring to the surface the material upon which our technological civilization rests. Certainly the two-fold activity of mind, conscious and subconscious, have been responsible for remaking the world.

Recently I stood on a bridge spanning the Tennessee River. This bridge overlooks historic Wilson Dam. Above this massive structure there is a reservoir of millions of tons of water. Just below the dam there is a power station. This station contains a dynamo capable of generating millions of volts of electric energy. At a necessary point in the dam there are channels through which the water held in the reservoir must flow to produce electrical energy. The complete mechanism for producing tremendous energy is ready to function. However, if the gates are not opened and channel the water to the power station, not one "erg" of energy is produced. The whole apparatus is completely useless unless it is set in motion. A demand must be made upon it for power. This is done by opening the gates and closing the right switch. Following this action, electric power goes out over the wires to run manufacturing plants, to light hundreds of thousands of homes and, in general, to make possible our modern way of life.

If a person does not know that this appartus for producing power exists, or, if a person is told that it does exist but refuses to believe that the statement is true, the potential energy available to him will be of no use whatever.

We have within our personalities the source of power, creative energy, that can be directed by actions of the conscious mind. This potential personal energy exists whether it is recognized or not. It is also inescapable for the conscious mind not to direct the activity of this underlying creative power. For this creative energy of mind to bring about the conditions desired by a person, it must be consciously and purposefully directed. Unless the right directions are given to the subconscious, its undirected activity may result in frustration, defeat and anxiety. No individual can escape the responsibility for the conditions under which he finds himself. It is simply a matter of the conscious mind selecting a constructive objective and then giving to the creative aspect of personality the proper direction empowered by hope and expectancy.

Our deep subconscious is a wonderland of mystery. This part of mind contains a summary and reservoir of race memory and accumulated skills. These skills and insight may be transmitted biologically from generation to generation in the original chromosomes of germ plasma.

The deeply submerged part of our mind is the powerhouse from which radiate the majestic intuitions of religion and the illuminating inspirations of artistic genius. In this same area of mind is found the foundation source of the most august insights of modern science. The most profound generalizations of philosophy also emerge from this same psyche reservoir. It is also from this same area of mind that the direction and content of the ordinary experiences of life are determined.

For the purpose of this book the terms conscious and subconscious mind will be employed. Various terms have been used by different writers in describing aspects of mind activity. Following Freud, the most commonly used term is "the unconscious." If this term simply indicates mental activity below the level of awareness in the conscious mind, it is correctly descriptive of this part of mental activity; however, if it is used to describe a blind process which is not aware of its own activity, it is misleading. Other terms are preconscious, fringe conscious and bioconscious. Certain writers have used three terms—the conscious mind, with its usual implications; the subconscious, to indicate the instinctive drives growing out of body processes; and the superconscious mind, to indicate the higher levels of mental activity, such as intuition, inspiration, etc. This study makes the assumption that mind is a unit and that the different levels of activity are parts of a unitary process. The varied activities of mind may well give the impression that mind itself is more like a spectrum than a monad; however, the complete picture indicates the essential unitary character of mind. The use of these terms—conscious mind and subconscious mind—in no way indicates that we possess two minds.

Previously I have described the function and relation of conscious and subconscious mind in the following paragraphs.[2]

"First consider that aspect of the mind known as the conscious or objective mind. This is the part of mind which makes decisions and exercises the power of choice. It has the ability to select, to discriminate between what is desired and what is not desired. It is that part of the mind which sits in judgment. It determines what we want or desire, and it initiates action to secure results. The conscious mind knows persons, things and conditions.

"The significant thing about the conscious mind, it should be

[2] John K. Williams, *The Knack of Using Your Subconscious Mind* (Englewood Cliffs, N.J.: Prentice-Hall, Inc.).

stressed, is its selectivity, or power of choice and decision. By its own nature, and because of this nature, the conscious mind can decide what it wants to think, what it wants to achieve, and how it will respond to other minds. It is the supreme determining and volitional aspect of personality.

"In ordinary language, the conscious mind is that which one speaks of when a person speaks of his 'self' but a fuller understanding will indicate that the conscious mind is not the total self, but only one aspect of the self or personality.

"Every object or condition must first exist in mind. Before any idea or plan can be formed, or any result achieved, it must first exist as an idea or concept in the conscious mind. Whether we realize it or not, all our lives we work from a series of mental pictures or blueprints. Making blueprints is the function of the conscious mind. In the exercise of this power the direction and content of one's life is determined.

"Before a bridge is built the architect must make a blueprint. Every detail of the proposed structure, its location, its size and weight, its relation to its surroundings, the material of which it is to be built—all these are visualized completely and in detail in the conscious mind of the architect and reduced to a blueprint before the engineers begin the process of construction.

"This is not only true of bridges and buildings; it is true of everything that comes into and forms a part of our experience. In general terms, the conscious mind may be thought of as the architect and the subconscious mind as the construction engineer."

William James, the famous teacher and psychologist of Harvard, once said that the greatest discovery in a hundred years was the discovery of the subconscious mind. In a very real sense, recognition of the fact that the subconscious aspect of mind can be directed and controlled by the conscious part of the mind may indeed be the greatest discovery of all time. The use of the subconscious indicates that man has within himself the power to control his surroundings, that he is not at the mercy of chance or luck, but that he can by the proper direction and control of the subconscious become the arbiter of his own fortune and thus carve out his own destiny. By proper methods he can be the master of the creative subconscious energy within his own life.

Freud, in his book *The Unconscious*, states that "our most intimate daily experience introduces us to sudden ideas of the source of which we are ignorant, and to results of mentation arrived at we know not how."

The great Swiss psychologist, Carl J. Jung, in his *Psychology and Religion* says, "The subconscious mind is capable at times of assuming an intelligence and purposiveness which are superior to actual conscious insight."

Another authority, Dr. Leon J. Saul, states, "Since Freud, it has been fully established that consciousness and even the conscious ego functions are, in a sense, only surface phenomena, however important they may be for adaption and for man's development. They are like the protruding tip of an iceberg, of which the main mass extends into the depths broad and deep." [3]

The conscious mind may not know how the subconscious works or feels, but the subconscious knows to the last detail and shade of feeling just what is in the conscious mind. The subconscious may overflow and its message not be understood by the conscious mind, but the reverse is never true. To control the functioning of the subconscious, the conscious mind must first honestly feel and believe that wisdom and insight necessary for the solution of the problem is available. The method—the how and why of the answer —is the responsibility of the subconscious mind.

There are two significant facts regarding the subconscious mind that are little understood, hence are unappreciated and unused by most of us. The first is that the subconscious mind contains within itself the power to create. The second is that the subconscious mind does at all times obey the orders given to it by the conscious mind. For, unlike the conscious mind, the subconscious mind has no power of choice. By its very nature it must do what it is told to do. Its function or purpose is that of bringing to full expression whatever is desired by the higher or self-conscious aspect of our mind.

[3] Leon J. Saul, M.D., *The Bases of Human Behavior* (Philadelphia: J. B. Lippincott Co.). Used by permission.

While the conscious mind is a law unto itself, deciding what it desires and determining its own destiny, the subconscious mind is impersonal and acts only in keeping with its own nature, that of serving the purpose of the conscious mind. Its content, its work, and its expression are determined, not by itself, but by that which is given to it to work on by the higher level of consciousness. It receives, retains and creates. Nothing which has once been given by the conscious mind to the subconscious mind to work on can be removed or expelled except by the action of the conscious mind itself. This reconditioning or the expelling of ideas or attitudes from the subconscious usually requires efforts over a period of time.

The subconscious mind is not only a storeroom; it is an area of infinite creative activity. The purpose of its activity is to give form and experience to that which it receives from the conscious mind. The subconscious is imaginative and inventive. It never grows weary. It is the willing servant of the man or woman who understands it, and intelligently uses his or her conscious mind to direct it.

The importance of the subconscious mind is indicated by Dr. Edmund W. Sinnott of Yale University—"He (man) is no mere glorified robot, ruthlessly weighing everything in the scales of survival and physical satisfaction. He is a vast deal more than a bundle of purposes with an intellect to help accomplish them. From far down within him, in that deep subconscious matrix where matter and energy and life are inextricably mixed together, there surge up into consciousness a throng of emotions, longings, loves and hates, imaginings and aspirations, some exalted and some base, which form the most important of what he is." [4]

Frederic W. H. Myers stated that the achievements of any man of genius "are the products of ideas which he has not consciously originated but which have shaped themselves in profounder regions of his being."

The conscious mind is limited by time and space but the sub-

4 Edmund W. Sinnott, *Cell and Psyche* (Chapel Hill, N.C.: University of North Carolina Press). Used by permission.

conscious mind is not limited by these measurements. Under proper conditions, the subconscious mind may accomplish instantaneously results which the conscious mind would require days, months or or even years to bring about. It was Freud who said that "the unconscious (subconscious) knows nothing of reason or logic."

The subconscious mind directs and sustains the vital processes and functions of life. Consider the indescribable complexity of the human body. Think of the eons of time which have been necessary for its development. Contemplate the marvelous chemical processes which begin at the moment of conception and continue until the end of our physical life.

The human heart beats, on the average, seventy times a minute, 100,800 times a day, and ten billion times in a life span of eighty years. The heart generates sufficient energy every twenty-four hours to lift a weight of sixty-five tons twelve feet in the air.

Each kidney has about 1,200,000 nephrons, each about two inches long, so that the combined length of all nephrons in an adult would amount to seventy-five miles. The total of all capillaries in both kidneys would measure more than thirty-seven miles. The entire filtering surface within the kidneys exceeds twice the body surface.

In an adult there are approximately 300,000,000 alveoli in both lungs with an aggregate surface of 700 square feet. The adult absorbs more than twenty cubic feet of oxygen in twenty-four hours, and the blood releases more than twenty cubic feet of carbon dioxide within the same period.

There are about twelve billion cells in your brain. While an electric current in a wire travels 11,160,000 miles a minute, the nerve impulses in the brain move with a speed of not more than four and one-half miles per minute. Remember, if all the equipment of the telegraph, radar and radio of North America could be squeezed into a half-gallon cup and continue to function, it would be simple compared to the work of the three pints of brain that fills your skull and mine.

At the end of the first embryonic month the human body is

about 8,000 times as heavy as at the moment of conception. Yet, during a life span of seventy years the body multiples its weight at birth, on the average, only twenty times.

The bloodstream of the human body is like a busy river. In it float countless billions of tiny ships, with many different shapes and tasks. They carry the wonderful elements of life to all tissues and cells of the body.

The blood constantly bathes all parts of the body. In each human body this transportation system is about 60,000 miles long. From the heart, the flood flows along the arteries to smaller arteries that reach all parts of your body. To them the blood ships carry oxygen, food and water. They carry hormones, the chemical messengers made by ductless glands. They distribute vitamins. They transport some of the enzymes—the chemicals involved—like a parson, in the marriage of other chemicals by which your body cells use food, grow, and carry on their jobs. Every minute these ships sail along, dropping off their cargoes at exactly the right time and places in your body.

These "ships of state" pick up waste products from the body tissues. Returning they flow along the veins, unloading or reloading. By comparison, man's best-run railroads are a bungling madhouse.

These mysterious and indescribably complex processes are controlled and directed by the subconscious mind. Modern medical science stands in awe of the wisdom and power displayed in these processes. It is in contemplating the physiologic and glandular processes of the human body that we find our greatest supporting data for the assumption that the subconscious area of mind has at its disposal infinite wisdom and power. In the words of the Psalmist, we, indeed, are "fearfully and wonderfully made."

The creative process of life is exhibited in the mysterious, goal-achieving activity of body cells. The human mind cannot explain the speed, precision and balance attained in the production of blood cells. Red corpuscles are manufactured in the marrow of the long bones at the rate of about 10,000,000 every second of every minute during the life span. The white blood cells, on the other hand, have a super wisdom in the presence of danger. These cells, which consume invading bacteria, multiply with terrific speed when infection enters the body.

To lay persons there are mere "cells," but scientists know that each cell is a living individual and performs its functions more intelligently than most human beings. Dr. Magnus Pyke, in his book, *The Boundaries of Science,* poses an interesting question regarding the creative, purposeful wisdom displayed by cells—"The most complex phenomenon in biology is the single fertilized cell which divides, and divides again, and yet again, and which produces here and there as the later cells in their turn divide into specialized cells and structures—livers, kidneys, hair, muscles—until at last the full complexity of a fruit fly, or a mouse, or a hedgehog, or a man stands before you. *How does the original cell know how to do this?*"

These cells have body, brain and nervous system. They respond not only to chemical stimulation, but also to mental and emotional impulses. To direct and sustain these processes and activities is obviously a task beyond the ability of the busy conscious mind.

One simply begs the question by saying that these and other still more complex processes are a "natural" function of the body. Back of nature, or law (chemical or otherwise), stand mind and intelligence. By all moral standards such variety and complexity require infinite mind, or intelligence. Conscious mind, of and by itself, is narrowly limited. Only that large area of personality known as the subconscious is equal to the gigantic task of keeping the body going and meeting the varied and complex situations it must weather if we are to survive.

We must keep definitely in mind, first of all, that the subconscious is the oldest part of the mind. The individual is subconscious mind long before he is conscious mind. Every biologist knows that our five senses were developed from an "original diffused and general sensitivity" which in very early stages must have been somewhat like the sense of touch. The subconscious mind is the development and adaption of this mind stuff brought about by millions of years of "trial-and-error" experience.

If one is to make significant use of the energy of the submerged area of the subconscious mind, he must keep in the forefront of his thinking this one fact: The energy of the submerged area of mind is subject to the orders of the conscious mind. In this sense the conscious mind is like a navigator directing the course of his ship. He sends orders to the men in the engine room who do not know where they are going but who follow the orders of the navigator. If the man who driects the course of the ship gives the wrong orders, if he fails to read correctly his instruments, then, delay or possible disaster will follow. The orders which the conscious mind sends down to the engine room of personality must have meaning and must represent what the conscious mind wants to accomplish and believes that it can accomplish.

The fact that we are unable to form a conception of the ultimate nature of mind does not mean that we cannot direct its activities. The human personality is similar to the far-reaching depth of the Mammouth Cave in the state of Kentucky. One enters this underground world with a tiny flickering lamp which provides illumination step by step as the caverns of the cave are explored. The exploration of this mysterious underground world must be made step by step. No beam of illumination will at one time reveal the many complex structures found in this cave. Point by point and step by step, the appreciation of its grandeur and majesty must be attempted.

The exploration and direction of subconscious activity are in some degree comparable to this. Each forward step by the conscious mind brings new light and understanding into areas previously not known. Thoughtful persons facing the complexities and confusions of life are beginning to realize the significance and importance of the subconscious area of mind.

There are numerous examples of creative work accomplished by men who moved through their activities with leisure and balance. The scientist, Alfred Russell Wallace, would go for days and weeks feeling no desire or interest in work. During these periods he occupied himself with his garden or simply by reading a novel. Then, a sudden impulse would come bringing him an explanation, a theory, a discovery, the plan of a book, and this impulse usually came to him like a flash of light. Subconscious activity generally brought with it not only plans but the material, the arguments and the illustrations necessary.

Thomas Edison did most of his creative work at night. Henry Cobb, the millionaire fruit packer, once said that all the really important ideas which helped him to build his business arrived in his mind at night while lying in bed. The great Frenchman, Voltaire frequently spent as much as fifteen to sixteen hours in bed, calling his secretary when there was anything to be committed to writing. Elbert Hubbard declared that his most important ideas came to him while working in his garden or riding horseback.

Intense activity of the conscious mind prevents the recognition of subconscious insight. Examine the origins of the great masterpieces of literature, art and music. Study the beginning of mental processes that have led to great inventions and new chemical processes; in short, study all those advances of our technological civilization and you will find that the new *insight*, the fuller understanding and integration, emerged from the field of subconscious activity during moments of relaxation and rest. The great and useful secrets of nature, as well as those intuitions which bring us peace of mind and soul, rarely arrive when we are traveling at supersonic speed.

> Know then thyself, presume not God to scan,
>   The proper study of mankind is man.
> A being darkly wise, and rudely great:
>   Born but to die and reasoning but to err;
> Sole judge of truth, in endless error hurled:
>   The glory, the jest and riddle of the world!

("Essay on Man," Alexander Pope)

4

THE CREATIVE
PROCESS AND THE
SUBCONSCIOUS

IT is now an accepted datum in psychology that the conscious mind is just the "emergent apex," the top level of an enormous and sustaining subconscious. Research has shown that the ability to bring into action this deeper area of the mind determines the success of every creative worker—scientists, author, musician, inventor, or business leader.

During the past sixty years more progress has been made in basic and applied research than was achieved during all previous centuries. Modern civilization in its structure and achievement rests upon a foundation built by subconscious activity in the fields of science, invention, music, the arts, and literature. From the time of Socrates, the founder of ethical science, to the inventive genius of Edison, Ford, Marconi, Westinghouse, Einstein and Kettering, this little understood and unrecognized area of mental activity has delivered the insight and know-how for almost every great achievement which makes possible and sustains modern civilization as we know it.

How Basic Concepts Arrive

Without the central concept of the theory of evolution, the modern intellectual climate would be a miasma of confusion. Charles

Darwin, after years of investigation and observation, accumulated data which he believed pointed to a new and significant insight regarding the processes of nature. Near the end of his life in a brief autobiographical statement he records, "I can remember the very spot in the road whilst in my carriage when to my joy the whole solution came to me." During the same period A. R. Wallace, who shares with Darwin the achievement of discovering the theory of evolution, had his first clear idea of this concept in his bed during an attack of malaria.

Of equal significance, in all probability the most important, is the concept of the modern period, the relationship of time and space, and the nature of physical reality which emerged into the mind of Albert Einstein while he relaxed in bed because of illness.

The subconscious mind selects its own times and the situations under which its insights are revealed. Newton discovered the Law of Gravitation while he relaxed under an apple tree. Urban civilization is possible because James Watt, who invented the steam engine, took a quiet walk on a Sunday afternoon. The idea which made possible rail locomotion developed in his mind with compelling clarity as his mind relaxed during his Sabbath walk.

Sir J. A. Thompson, in a recent presidential address to the British Association, mentioned that the solution of some of his most intricate problems came to him when he emptied his mind of the problems and let it remain quiet and still for a time.

The November 11, 1962, issue of *This Week* magazine carried the story of a scientific instrument that can light up the moon, kill instantly, or perform miracle surgery.

This scientific instrument, known as the "laser," resulted from a brain storm of Dr. Charles H. Townes, then a thirty-five-year-old physics professor at Columbia University. It was a spring morning in 1951, and Dr. Townes was sitting on a park bench in Washington. He was thinking of the problem of microwaves physics. At that time an idea from his subconscious mind emerged in his train of thought. This subconscious idea, while its full potential has not been developed, has resulted in dramatic achievements.

In a laboratory at Schenectady a group of General Electric engineers recently pointed a small instrument about the size of a basketball at a diamond, pulled the trigger and burned a hole through the diamond in 200 millionths of a second.

Another group of scientists at Lexington, Massachusetts, from Massachusetts Institute of Technology and the Raytheon Company, pointed the same type of device at the darkened moon. A two-mile square on the moon was clearly illuminated by this flash of "coherent waves." The time required was exactly 1.3 seconds. For the first time in history, man had illuminated a distant planet.

As to the miracle surgery, its dramatic power was demonstrated in a hospital in New York. Doctors working with a ruby laser projected a ruby pulse for one-thousands of a second through the lens of the eye of a patient. The single flash was aimed at a tumor on the retina, the rear wall of the eye on which images register. The tumor disappeared.

Such are the immediate but not final results of an instrument developed because of the intrusion of subconscious insight into the conscious mind of a physics professor, sitting on a park bench in our national capital.

The Russian, Prince Kropotkin, had for several years been intently interested in the physical conformation of Asia. He writes in his memoirs that he had marked on a large-scale map all geological and physical observations that had been made by different travelers and that he had tried to find out what structural lines would answer the observed realities. This preparatory work required over two years. Then followed months of intense thought in order to find out what the bewildering chaos of scattered observations meant, until one day all of a sudden the whole became as clear and comprehensible "as if it were illumined with a flash of light."

Von Helmholtz, the German physicist, speaking on his seventieth birthday, described the way in which his most important new thoughts had come to him. He said that after previous investigation of a problem "in all directions . . . happy ideas come unexpectedly without effort, like an inspiration. So far as I am concerned they have never come to me when my mind was fatigued or when I was at my working table." Helmholtz found that rest was necessary for the appearance of scientific inspiration and that brilliant ideas often occurred to him in the morning after a night's rest.

The answer may come during one's awakening moments, or it may arrive unannounced at any time of the day. Descartes, the French mathematician and philosopher, is said to have made his great discoveries while lying in bed in the morning.

Said Thomas Edison, who himself contributed so much to progress, "The key to successful methods comes right out of the air. A real, new thing like an idea, a beautiful melody, is pulled out of space."

The distinguished research scientist, Dr. Irving Langmuir, recently said: "We often underrate the importance of intuition. In almost every scientific problem which I have succeeded in solving, even those that have involved days or months of work, the final solution has come to my mind in a fraction of a second by a process which is not consciously one of reasoning."

The French mathematician, Henri Poincare, described his creative work in almost the same terms. He stated that creative ideas did not come to him while he worked at his desk, but frequently flashed into his mind while he engaged in other activities.

Dr. W. H. Rivers, the well-known psychologist, stated that many of the scientific ideas he valued most, as well as the language in which they were expressed, came to him in the "half-sleeping, half-waking" state directly continuous with definite sleep.

The Creative Process in Research and Invention

Recently Platt and Baker reported in the Journal of Chemical Education the result of a survey among 1,450 chemists engaged in research. This group represented the leading research laboratories as well as the large chemical manufacturing industries of the nation. All major advances of the chemical industry during the previous thirty years resulted from the insight and skill of these men.

The carefully prepared questionnaire asked these research scientists to describe how and when new ideas and rewarding insights arrived. For example, did the new ideas emerge while they were actively studying data related to their unsolved problem? Was the solution to the problem found in the laboratory during routine work? Did the new concept result from a process of careful, cogent reasoning, or did the new insight occur as a sudden flash—"a hunch," a full-grown plan from the deeper levels of mind? More replies were received than were necessary to make the conclusions formulated by Platt and Baker valid.

In practically every instance these men replied that new insight and solutions rarely came while they were working in the laboratory, or while consciously engrossed in the study of data related to the problem. Far more than a majority of these men reported that their discoveries came in moments of relaxation following upon weeks or months of intensive application. The solution to their problems did not arrive as the result of cold logical reasoning, but arrived in consciousness full and complete at off moments and under varying circumstances.

An outstanding scientist stated that the idea for a great advance came when, "freeing my mind of all thoughts of the problem I walked down Tremont Street . . . when as if from the clear sky above me an idea popped into my head suddenly." In another instance, the needed insight emerged, "while riding on a train." Another reporting member of the group found the solution to his problem while "sitting at my desk doing nothing and thinking of other matters."

One significant fact stands out in this survey: Ideas occur in the most unorthodox fashion. One man had an idea that resulted in a significant change in a manufacturing process, "while dodging automobiles crossing Park Row and Broadway." In another instance, a member of the group found the solution to his problem, "while dressing after bathing in the sea." Other members of the group made discoveries and solved problems in various ways and, at times, results were not anticipated: "in bed at three o'clock in the morning"; "Sunday morning in church while the preacher was reading his text." For other members of the group, new ideas came while shaving and dressing, gardening, fishing, playing solitaire, and while walking between their homes and offices. The subconscious part of the mind works continuously night and day. Apparently it must find a period when the conscious mind is relaxed—certainly when it is not engaged in intensive work—to report the results of its mentation.

In this report two instances of the immediate practical value of subconscious activity are given. "The wheel from earliest time until October, 1929, was a structure designed empirically—even the wire wheels of the automobile. In my standardization work for our company, it was desirable to control the design technically—as we have many designers who work on this problem. We now make and use over 1,000 different kinds of wheels—over 1,500,000 wheels a year, at a manufacturing cost of over $10,000,000. In order to make a huge saving which nets about $2,000,000 a year, the importance of the technical wheel was evident. Therefore, as chairman of the wheel committee, I found no guiding data in textbooks, etc., and had to make a solution. After trying vainly to get one by regular well-known application of mechanics over ten months, I suddenly got a "hunch" which, after four and one-half hours of application thereafter, proved the correctness of the suggestion and this resulted in a beautiful new solution which has proved itself correct in every detail on research tests, as well as practical tests."

Another researcher states, "I remember distinctly, while head of the laboratories of the old _____ Company, working on a problem that had bothered them for years (probably 15 or 20 years). We worked on it quite intensively for several months; and after that only occasionally. One day while sitting at my desk doing nothing, and thinking about other matters, a thought flashed through my mind. I immediately left the office, went out into the plant by myself, made a few tests, and solved the difficulty. I then went to the manager and told him about it and he would not believe it until I showed him some samples, as it seemed to be too simple. I have had the same thing happen since then at different times, but never quite so pronounced as at that time or on a problem upon which we had worked for so long a time unsuccessfully." [1]

In general, discoveries were made after full investigation and evaluation of the problem, exhaustive study of all data, then change and relaxation. These scientists revealed a close spiritual kinship with Archimedes who solved the problem of specific gravity while relaxed in his morning bath.

The Creative Process in Medical Research

Many of the most important facts found in medical literature today were made known by subconscious mentation. The circulation of blood in the human body is such an obvious fact that we forget it was not always recognized as a part of our physical routine. After years of study and thinking, the idea that the blood circulates through the human body arrived in the mind of Harvey from the deep submerged strata of mind. Another insight, which is one of the foundation stones of psychology and the behavioral sciences, is the significance of bodily changes in fear and rage. Dr. Walter E. Cannon, the first to state and provide supporting data, reports that "one wakeful night . . . the idea flashed through my mind." Alexis Carrel, one of the outstanding physiologists of the past generation, is reported to have received all his important thoughts and ideas while quietly walking during his summer vacations in his native Brittany.

Before October, 1920, medical science could offer no means of control or prevention for diabetes, the dreaded affliction of millions of people. At this time Frederick Grant Banting, in order to supplement the income from his meager private practice, was teaching in the University of Toronto. During a particular night in October, 1920, young Banting was preparing his lecture for the following day. His subject was the then obscure affliction known as diabetes. Hour after hour Banting studied the literature on this disease. His mind was a maze of conflicting theories, case histories and records of experiments with dogs, which up until that time, had yielded little, if any, practical knowledge.

[1] Washington Platt and Ross A. Baker, *Journal of Chemical Education*, Vol. 8 No. 10, pp. 1,969–2,002.

Working late, he went to bed and at two o'clock in the morning he suddenly awoke. In his mind was a formula, which, when applied furnished a solution to his problem. This formula included three short sentences which he wrote in his notebook immediately after waking from sleep. "Tie off the pancreatic duct of dog. Wait six to eight weeks for degeneration. Remove residue and extract." Turning off the light he immediately went back to bed and to sleep. It was this briefly stated formula which led to the discovery of insulin. Banting's conscious mind had come to grips with one of the baffling problems of medical science but could find no solution. His subconscious mind delivered to his conscious mind the method by which life and hope were extended to millions of afflicted persons.

Observe that this young physician had been mentally and emotionally struggling with the problem of diabetes for many months. His mind was in a state of confusion because of conflicting theories, case histories and the records of animal experimentation. The significant fact is, that following full consideration of all available data, and while his conscious mind relaxed in sleep, his subconscious mind solved the problem.

Pasteur was accustomed, after he had dined each night, to pace the hall and corridor of his room at the École Normale meditating on the details of his work. New insights or discoveries are frequently made when one is engaged in work not related to the immediate problem.

As Charles Nicolle once said, "The longer you are in the presence of difficulty, the less likely you are to solve it." It is known that many important insights and concepts have arrived apparently by chance. Among such instances may be mentioned Fleming's understanding of the significance of penicillin. Another example is that of the French physiologist, Charles Richet, who discovered induced sensitization or anaphylaxis.

The same process is illustrated in the development of the origin of the idea of phagocytosis. Metchnokoff gives this account of this far-reaching insight:

One day when the whole family had gone to the circus to see some extraordinary performing apes, I remained alone with my microscope, observing the life in the mobile cells of a transparent starfish larva, when a new thought suddenly flashed across my mind. It struck me that similar cells might serve in the defense of the organism against intruders. Feeling that there was in this something of surprising interest, I felt so excited that I began striding up and down the room and even went to the seashore to collect my thoughts.[2]

Intuitions sometimes occur during sleep and a remarkable example is quoted by Cannon. Otto Loewi, professor of pharmacology at the University of Graz, awoke one night with a brilliant idea. He reached for a pencil and paper and jotted down a few notes. On waking the next morning he was aware of having an inspiration during the night, but to his consternation could not decipher his notes. All day at the laboratory in the presence of familiar apparatus he tried to remember the idea and to decipher the notes, but in vain. By bedtime he had been unable to recall anything, but during the night, to his great joy he again awoke with the same flash of insight. This time he carefully recorded it before going to sleep again. The next day he went to his laboratory and in one of the neatest, simplest and most definite experiments in the history of biology brought proof of the chemical mediation of nerve impulses. This was the beginning of a host of investigations in many countries throughout the world on chemical intermediation, not only between nerves and the muscles and glands they affect, but also between nerve elements themselves.[3]

The Creative Process in Music

"When I am, as it were, completely myself, entirely alone, and of good cheer: it is on such occasions that my ideas flow best and most abundantly, whence and how they come I know not, nor can

[2] B. M. Fried, *Archives of Pathology*, 1938.
[3] W. D. Cannon, M.D., *The Way of an Investigator* (New York: W. W. Norton & Company, Inc.). Used by permission.

I force them," Mozart confessed to a friend. Regarding his inspiration, Mozart said, "Nor do I hear in my imagination the parts in sequence, but I hear them, as it were, all at once. . . . What a delight that is I cannot tell."

Richard Wagner recorded that ideas for his muscial compositions came to him "like a flash of light in the greatest clarity and definiteness, but not altogether in complete detail." He discovered the opening of the Rheingold during "half-sleep" on a couch in the hotel at Spezia, and in a letter to Frau Wesendonk he refers to the blissful dream-state into which he falls when composing.

Beethoven clearly stresses the inadequacy of the rational mind for creativity. "The new and original is born of itself without one's thinking of it." With Chopin, creation was spontaneous, miraculous —he wrought without foreseeing. It would come complete, sudden, sublime. A new version of the *Third Symphony in C* came to Sir Hubert Parry quite suddenly as he lay trying to sleep on the afternoon of September 21, 1888.

Tchaikovsky wrote: "Generally speaking, the germ of a future composition comes suddenly and unexpectedly." Many of his themes were invented and his works planned during long solitary walks. It was the emerging of subconscious insights and creativity that the renowned French composer, Saint-Saens, was describing when he maintained that he had only to listen.

The treasury of all memories and experiences is in the subconscious mind. When it is highly sensitive and supernormally developed, we have a prodigy or genius—a Mozart or a Goethe. Often the creations of musicians, painters, writers and inventors are wholly the result of operations of the subconscious. In a book titled *The Poetic Mind*, Frederick Clarke Prescott asserts that poets have the ability for creativity while in a reverie-like state.

The Creative Process in Literature

One after another, the great writers, poets and artists confirm the fact that their work comes from beyond the threshold of consciousness. It is not as though this material came passively floating toward them. It is imperious, dynamic and willful. Blake said of one of his poems, *Milton*, "I have written this poem from immediate dictation, twelve or sometimes twenty or thirty lines at a time, without premeditation, and even against my will."

Keats said that the description of Apollo in the third book of *Hyperion* came to him "by chance or magic to be—as it were—something given." He said also that he had not been aware of the beauty of some thoughts or expressions until after he had composed and written the lines. It had then struck him with astonishment and seemed rather the production of another person than his own.

Wordsworth said that the line of the ode beginning, "Falling from us, vanishings," which has since puzzled so many readers, refers to those trance-like states to which he was at one time subject. During these moments the world around him seemed unreal and the poet had occasionally to use his strength against an object, such as a gatepost, to reassure himself. And when the power would not come, the conscious mind was helpless.

Dickens declared that when he sat down to write, "Some beneficent power showed it all to me." And Thackeray says in the *Roundabout Papers*, "I have been surprised at the observation made by some of my characters. It seems as if an occult Power was moving my pen."

The Indian poet and mystic, Tagore, was once interviewed about his poetry and his creative method. Tagore said, "I believe that each one of us has two beings within him. One of these is quite above the other in intelligence and feeling. This is the unconscious self. The other being, the conscious self, is quite a stupid fellow. If this stupid conscious self gets the ascendary, nothing is accomplished. But if we can only take this stupid conscious fellow and hold him in subjection, and not let him interfere with our unconscious self, then we can reach heights seemingly unattainable."

Oliver Wendell Holmes has presented this undoubted fact clearly and convincingly: "I will give some instances of work done in the underground workshop of thought. We wish to remember something in the course of conversation—no effort of the will can reach it—but we say, "Wait a minute and it will come to me," and go on talking. Presently, some minutes later, the idea we are in search of comes all at once into the mind, delivered like a prepared bundle, laid at the door of consciousness, like a foundling in a basket. How it came there, we know not. The mind must have been at work groping and feeling for it in the dark, it cannot come by itself. Yet, all the while, our consciousness, so far as we are conscious of our consciousness, was busy with other thoughts . . . the more we examine the mechanism of thought, the more we shall see that automatic, unconscious action of the mind enters largely into all its processes. Our definite ideas are stepping-stones; how we get from one to another we do not know. . . . Persons who talk most do not always think most, I question whether persons who think most, that is, have most conscious thought pass through their minds—necessarily do the most mental work."

George Eliot, in a letter to a friend said, "I am writing a story which came across my other plans by a sudden inspiration." Vincent van Gogh once said that he had "a terrible lucidity at moments, when nature is so glorious in those days I am hardly conscious of myself and the picture comes to me like a dream." Thomas Hardy recalled how, when wandering about the countryside, ideas often came into his mind when he had not a scrap of paper upon him.

William Blake, the English artist and poet, did his immortal work while his subconscious was in complete control.

Sir Walter Scott declared that the half-hour between waking and rising had always been propitious to any composition he had in mind. When he had any difficulty, a knotty problem in a story, or a passage in a poem to fill in, it was always when first he awoke in the morning that the desired ideas came to him. "This is so much the case," Scott declared, "that I am in the habit of relying upon it, and saying to myself when I am at a loss, 'Never mind, we shall have it at seven o'clock tomorrow morning.' "

Bertrand Russell said, "My own belief is that a conscious thought can be planted in the unconscious if a sufficient amount of vigor and intensity is put into it. Most of the unconscious consists of what were once highly emotional conscious thoughts, which have now become buried. It is possible to do this process of burying deliberately, and in this way the unconscious can be led to do a lot of useful work. I have found, for example, that, if I have to write upon some rather difficult topic, the best plan is to think about it with very great intensity—the greatest intensity of which I am capable—for a few hours or days, and at the end of that time give orders, so to speak, that the work is to proceed underground. After some months I return consciously to the topic and find that the work has been done." [4]

The following paragraph describes the way Metternich, the great Austrian statesman, used—and implicitly depended upon—his subconscious mind; and the efficiency of the leisurely, confident approach. It is interesting to note the way in which his mind worked in solving a problem. "The necessary results mature rapidly," he said, "under apparent distractions. While eating, in ordinary conversation or in riding, the clearest revelations and the most important ideas come. As soon as the object has ripened quite lucidly within me and my mind and spirit are saturated with it, I put it upon paper, unworried about order and sequence, which then arrange themselves of their own accord." His private physician, Dr. Jaeger, tells that Metternich had just returned from a wearisome night's journey when he was met by a courier with an important dispatch. The courier asked what the answer was to be. Metternich replied, "I really do not know yet. Let me first finish the novel in my travel bag. Perhaps the answer will come."

The following statement of Tennyson describes the mood or emotional state in which creative energy in any of the arts seems to function. He writes: "A kind of waking trance I have frequently had, quite up from boyhood, when I have been all alone. . . . All at once, as it were, the intensity of the consciousness of the individuality, the individuality itself, seemed to dissolve and fade away into boundless being; and this is not a confused state, but the clearest of the clearest, the surest of the surest, utterly beyond words, when death was an almost laughable impossibility, the loss of personality seeming no extinction, but the only true life. I am

[4] Bertrand Russell, *The Conquest of Happiness* (New York: Liveright Publishing Corp.). Used by permission.

ashamed of my feeble description. Have I not said the state was utterly beyond words?"

In George Meredith, we find this tribute to the same fundamental wisdom when he speaks of "those instantaneous bolts of passionate perception, which flash a livid furrow across the eyeballs of the brain, leaving them momentarily blind to the outer universe, only to quicken the scene of inward and incommunicable things."

The late Gutzon Borglum, renowned as a sculptor, once said that his most creative period came usually late in the afternoon, when he had done what he could, and worn himself to a frazzle with his conscious mind. Then something from his subconscious would usually emerge.

Robert Ingersoll used to construct his eloquent lectures while whistling loudly and playing billiards. That was his technique for occupying his conscious and liberating his subconscious. Henry Ward Beecher used to occupy his conscious mind by taking clocks to pieces and putting them together while he was composing his eloquent sermons.

Novelist Louis Bromfield comments, "One of the most helpful discoveries I made long ago in common with some other writers is that there is a part of the mind, which the psychologists call the 'subconscious,' that works while you are sleeping or even while you are relaxing or engaged in some other task far removed from writing. I have found it possible to train this part of the mind to do a pretty organized job. Very often I have awakened in the morning to find a problem of technique, or plot, or character, which has long been troubling me, completely solved while I had been sleeping. The judgment of the 'subconscious mind' which represents inherited instincts and the accumulation of experience, is virtually infallible, and I would always trust its decision over any judgment arrived at through a long and reasonable process of conscious thinking."

The Creative Process in Business

Oliver Wendell Holmes once spoke of subconscious activity as "the underground workshop of thought." Since the subconscious mind works from a deductive rather than an inductive reasoning process, the insights which are received from this aspect of the mind have the ability to recognize analogies and appreciate the significance of apparently accidental, unrelated facts. Every successful businessman, as well as every creative thinker, knows the experience Lamartine had in mind when he said, "It is not I who thinks. It is my ideas that think for me."

A former president of the National Broadcasting Company, Lenox Riley Lohr, once described how ideas which had helped him in his business arrived: "Ideas, I find, come most readily when you are doing something that keeps the mind alert without putting too much strain upon it. Shaving, driving a car, sawing a plank, or fishing or hunting, for instance. Or engaged with some friends in stimulating conversation. Some of my best ideas came from information picked up casually and entirely unrelated to my work."

The experience of William Gibbs McAdoo, Secretary of the Treasury under President Woodrow Wilson, is typical of the mental habits of many outstanding business and political leaders. When McAdoo retired, usually about midnight, he consciously turned his affairs over to his subconscious mind and went to sleep. As is always the case, his subconscious mind continued to work on the problem with which he had been concerned during the day. He placed a tablet and pencil near his bed and would be awakened several times during the night by reports from his subconscious mind. It was his habit to jot down words or symbols to help him recall these upswings of insight which came during the night.

Dr. Elmer Gates is well known as an inventor and research authority. Gates refined and perfected more than 200 patents which other inventors had undertaken but which had fallen short of success. He was able to add the missing ingredient, the something more. His method was to begin by examining the application for the patent until he found its weakness, the element that was lacking. He would bring a copy of the patent application and drawing into his study and while "sitting for ideas" he would concentrate to find a solution for the specific problem.

The well-known writer, Napoleon Hill, in an interview asked Dr. Gates to explain the sources of the results which he achieved "while sitting for ideas." In reply Dr. Gates stated that "the sources of all ideas are:

1. Knowledge stored in the subconscious mind and acquired through individual experience, observation and education.

2. Knowledge accumulated by others through the same media, which may be communicated by telepathy.

3. The great universal storehouse of Infinite Intelligence, wherein is stored all knowledge and all facts, and which may be contacted through the subconscious section of the mind.

Napoleon Hill, who was associated with Robert G. LeTourneau, outstanding industrial leader, for eighteen months and had an opportunity to observe him closely, tells of an incident which occurred after LeTourneau had become a well-known inspirational lecturer. He devoted much of his time to traveling around the country in his private plane, preaching his message: "It's wonderful to be in partnership with God." One night when the two men were flying home from a speaking engagement in North Carolina, something interesting happened. Soon after his pilot took off, Mr. LeTourneau went to sleep. In about thirty minutes Napoleon Hill saw him take a little notebook from his pocket and write several lines in it. After the plane landed Mr. Hill asked Mr. LeTourneau if he remembered writing in his notebook. "Why no!" exclaimed Mr. LeTourneau. He immediately pulled the notebook from his pocket and looked in it. He said, "Here it is! A problem that has kept me from completing a machine we are working on." [5]

One should recognize the fact that there is a definite distinction between daydreaming and the goal-directed use of the subconscious. Daydreamers who imagine themselves performing feats of heroic strength, keeping a room full of people entertained with their brilliant remarks and suddenly finding themselves directing a great

[5] Napoleon Hill and W. Clement Stone, *Success Through a Positive Mental Attitude* (Englewood Cliffs, N.J.: Prentice-Hall, Inc.). Used by permission.

business enterprise, are wasting their time in useless, undirected wishful thinking. They are simply making an escape from their own mediocrity and lack of intelligent purpose. Correctly employed, subconscious mentation on the other hand reveals new aspects of one's problem, permits one to visualize himself as actually accomplishing his purpose and, from a standpoint of his emotional drive, furnishes the motivation for successful work.

In this chapter it has only been possible to present a very small part of the data available regarding subconscious inspiration and creative work. A full investigation would show that all people who do creative work receive their basic insights as the result of subconscious mentation.

5

"SLEEP ON IT"— DREAMS AND THE SUBCONSCIOUS

THE subconscious mind is the great storehouse of life. Every thought and every feeling that we have ever experienced, our so-called instincts, the wisdom born of thousands of years of man's struggle and development, form a part of our subconscious endowment. From the standpoint of its historical development, the subconscious has within itself the limitless ability and skill which mankind has developed through many thousands of years.

As one of the ancient philosophers stated, the subconscious aspect of mind is a "blind force, not knowing, only doing." It is working all the time but with most of us it works without intelligent, conscious direction. As we learn to use it consciously and constructively we shall add greatly to our control over ourselves and give greater focus and motivation to our lives.

A very significant and interesting fact about the subconscious is that within its structure is found a complete memory picture of every thought, action and emotional tone we have experienced during our lifetime. The subconscious is the sleepless recording angel of our personalities. Under proper conditions a person can recall in detail the events of his life, going back to the day of birth. Certainly there is sound experimental evidence that the subconscious records and retains many times more rapidly and completely than the conscious mind.

To understand fully the creative activity of the subconscious mind, we must consider the significant insights and the solution of difficult problems as revealed by subconscious processes through dreams. In a deep hypnotic state an individual can recall any incident in his past life. The hypnotic state is only a sleep-like condition, perhaps a kind of partial sleep, but in a different way normal sleep also releases the findings of this underlying aspect of mind.

When you go to sleep your conscious mind ceases its activity. The subconscious mind then takes control. While you sleep your subconscious mind talks to you, and this is what we call dreaming.

During past centuries among all peoples, dreams have been one of the channels through which subconscious wisdom has been delivered. In some instances subconscious mentation has served as a warning or premonition regarding occurrences in the future.

There is a tradition (apparently authentic) that Caesar's wife, Calpurnia, had a dream warning of danger on the night preceding the Ides of March. The Greek biographer, Plutarch, first recorded the story. He stated that Caesar was so impressed by his wife's fear and anxiety that he almost yielded to her insistence that he not go to the Senate. Had he refrained, history might have been different —certainly the world would not have that masterpiece of literature, *Julius Caesar*, by Shakespeare.

In his book about the life of the poet Dante, Boccaccio tells the story of a near tragedy so far as the literature of that period is concerned. After Dante's death several concluding cantos of the *Paradiso* could not be found. Every possible place for these manuscripts was examined by the poet's sons without success. Despairing of finding the lost materials, they attempted to write copy to complete the manuscript. Jacopo, one of Dante's sons, had a dream which caused them to discontinue this effort. In Jacopo's dream, his father led him to his old bedroom in another house where his recent death occurred. Touching one of the walls the poet said, "What you have sought for so much is here." The dream completed, Jacopo wide awake and with witnesses hurried to the house to which he had been led in the dream. Attached to one wall was a hanging frame which no one seems to have noticed during Dante's lifetime. Examining this frame they found a niche in the wall and in it the thirteen cantos needed to complete Dante's composition.

An interesting example of the premonitory type of subconscious insight which appears in dreams is found in the life of the woman suffragist leader, Susan B. Anthony. Miss Anthony's intimate friend, Elizabeth Cady Stanton, recorded in her diary:

> She has had a very remarkable dream. The physician ordered her from Philadelphia to Atlantic City for her health. While in the latter place, she had a very vivid dream one night. She thought she was being burnt alive in one of the hotels, and when she arose in the morning, told her niece what she had dreamed. "We must pack at once and go back to Philadelphia," she said. This was done, and the next day the hotel in which they had been and ten other hotels and miles of boardwalk were destroyed by fire.

It is well known that scientific inventions have been created as the result of dreams and difficult intellectual problems have been solved. Frank Podmore tells of an instance during which a long sought solution was vividly revealed to the sleeper not as a remembered dream, but was presented when the person became fully awake: "Professor Lamberton of the University of Pennsylvania records that after having vainly worked for some days with a geometrical problem, one morning immediately on waking he saw the solution given on the wall in front of his eyes."

Recently a friend of mine described an incident in which a difficult problem in mathematics was solved as the result of insight delivered in a dream. "While a senior in high school I was taking a course in advanced business arithmetic. One day the teacher was giving the assignment. He said, 'The next problem we shall omit. It is entirely too difficult for high school seniors.' Then, as an afterthought, he added, 'If any of you choose to work it and do so correctly, you will get an A on the course.'

"I simply could not let such a challenge go unaccepted. That night I worked until well past midnight trying in vain to get the answer. However, although I checked my work over and over, I finally despaired of finding the error which was responsible for my answer being unlike that given in the back of the book. Finally I decided to give up and try again the next day. I went to bed and to sleep. After an hour or so I suddenly awoke. There in the darkness of the night I knew immediately where my error had been, and I knew that it was the discovery of my error while sleeping that had awakened me. There was no need to get up and correct my error at the moment. So vivid was the revelation that I knew it would remain clear in my mind the following morning and then would be time enough to correct my work of the previous evening and make my A on the course. This is what I did." [1]

While it is recognized on every hand that the conscious part of mind is limited, the subconscious transcends the limitations of time and space. This is proved by well-attested experience related by many people under varying conditions.

During dreams the subconscious mind seems to have access to facts and information stored in the Universal Mind. This type of experience is reported by many creative writers and researchers. An example of this type of subconscious wisdom is found in the experience of Louis Agassiz, as told by his wife: "He had been striving to decipher the somewhat obscure impression of a fossil fish on the stone slab in which it was preserved. Weary and perplexed, he put his work aside and tried to dismiss it from his mind. Shortly after, he waked one night persuaded that while asleep he had seen his fish with all the missing features perfectly restored.

"He went early to the Jardin des Plantes, thinking that on looking anew at the impression he would see something to put him on the track of his vision. In vain—the blurred record was as blank as ever. The next night he saw the fish again, but when he waked it disappeared from his memory as before. Hoping the same experience might be repeated, on the third night he placed a pencil and paper beside his bed before going to sleep.

"Toward morning the fish reappeared in his dream, confusedly at first, but at last with such distinctness that he no longer had any doubt as to its zoological characters. Still half dreaming, in perfect

[1] (Percy M. Sessions, Clinic Administrator and author, Birmingham).

darkness, he traced these characters on the sheet of paper at his bedside.

"In the morning he was surprised to see in his nocturnal sketch features which he thought it impossible the fossil itself would reveal. He hastened to the Jardin des Plantes and, with his drawing as a guide, succeeded in chiseling away the surface of the stone under which portions of the fish proved to be hidden. When wholly exposed, the fossil corresponded with his dream and his drawing, and he succeeded in classifying it with ease."

This question of unusual information and intuition being delivered by dreams is in no way unusual. It is known that Poe's favorite literary work, "Ligeia" was suggested by a dream. The three opening stanzas of "A Vision of Spring in Winter" were given to Swinburne in a dream while in deep sleep. Tartini's violin sonata, "Trillo del Diavolo," came to him in a dream in which he imagined that the devil played upon his violin a composition of great beauty and strength. Mozart was recalling the same kind of subconscious mental activity when he wrote to a friend, "The process with me is like a vivid dream."

Take as an example the story of Dr. Herman V. Hilprecht, late professor of the Assyrian language at the University of Pennsylvania. During the winter of 1882–83, Dr. Hilprecht had exhausted himself trying to decipher the inscriptions on some old Assyrian rings. Finally he came to the conclusion that the task was impossible. One night he went to bed exhausted. While sleeping he dreamed. In his dream he saw a vision. A tall, stately priest of the ancient Pre-Christian Nippur Temple appeared before him and guided him to the treasure chamber of the temple. He entered a room with a low ceiling and without windows where his attention was directed by the priest to a wooden chest with scraps of agate and other articles lying on the floor around it.

Clearly and distinctly the priest of the temple said, "The fragments in which you are interested and for which you have been unable to find an explanation are not finger rings. The great king, Jurigalzu, once sent to the Temple of Bel an inscribed votive cylinder of agate. At a later period, the priest of the temple suddenly received an imperative command to make at once a pair of agate earrings for the god Nippur. The priests were greatly disturbed because no new agate was at hand. In order to obey the command it was decided to cut the votive cylinder into three parts, thus making three rings. The two fragments which have caused you so much mental anguish are parts of those rings. By placing them together you will find this to be true. The third ring you will never find." At this point Professor Hilprecht awoke and went hastily to his wife's room and told her of the dream. Then, with equal haste, he went to his study. Before long the professor's wife heard him exclaim, "It is so! It is so!"

The following winter Professor Hilprecht went to Cairo to study the objects of the Temple Nippur which had been placed in the Imperial Museum. After critical study based upon training and experience in the field of archeology, and his extended knowledge of the ancient languages, he came to the conclusion that the objects there furnished complete evidence of the correctness of his dream in every detail.[2]

Dr. Elwood Worcester was one of America's greatest religious psychiatrists. Twenty-five thousand nervous, tense, distraught people received treatment and counsel in his clinic in Boston. He was frequently overworked helping all these people while at the same time carrying on the work of a large church. He tells of going to bed one Friday night with the realization that he had not prepared a sermon for his congregation the following Sunday. Suffering from severe fatigue he felt unable to attack the job of preparation. That night he dreamed that a former assistant pastor, Dr. Walter Lowrie, came and reproached him for his failure to prepare. Then and there Dr. Lowrie dictated a sermon to Dr. Worcester, who wrote it down. The next morning when he awakened, he was disappointed that he did not have the inspiring sermon that he had dreamed about. Rising from his bed he saw some penciled sheets nearby. There was the sermon in his own handwriting. He had written it during the night while he slept. He delivered the sermon

[2] W. H. Myers, *Human Personality and Its Survival of Bodily Death* (New York: Longmans, Green & Co., Inc.).

and the response of his congregation was greater than usual. Later he included it in a volume called *Religion and Life*. When Dr. Lowrie read the sermon, he said he had never followed that particular line of thought in his life. Lowrie's seeming presence in the night was not a reality—but the sermon was.[3]

It will be recalled that James Watt was the inventor of the first practical steam engine—a machine which marked the start of a revolution in commerce and travel throughout the civilized world. James Watt made another contribution, perhaps less dramatic than the steam engine, but of great importance and he attributed this invention to a dream. During the period in which Watt lived, the making of lead shot for shotguns was a difficult and costly process, and in this process the results were frequently unsatisfactory.

While working on this problem James Watt began having the same dream night after night for a week. According to the account which Watt later gave of this dream, he seemed to be walking along in a heavy rainstorm, but instead of rain he would be showered with tiny leaden pellets that fell and rolled about his feet. Watt wondered what the significance of his dreams might be—did it by any chance mean that molten lead falling from the air would harden into tiny balls? He asked for permission to make experiments in the tower of a church which had a water-filled moat at the base. Melting a few pounds of lead, he tossed it out the belfry. To his astonishment when he recovered it from the water in the moat, he found that the lead had hardened into tiny round pellets. Since that time all lead shots have been made by the same process, which was discovered by Watt, and the source of his insight was a recurring dream.

Another equally interesting instance in which the invention was due to a dream is that of Elias Howe. Howe had been attempting to determine where the eye of the needle of a sewing machine should be located. Howe dreamed that the King gave him twenty-four hours to complete the machine so it would work, otherwise he was to be put to death. He worked and puzzled, and finally gave

---

[3] Lewis L. Dunnington, *Handle of Power* (Nashville, Tenn.: Abingdon Press). Used by permission.

it up. Then he thought they were leading him to the place where he was to be executed. He noticed that the warriors carried spears which were pierced near the head. Instantly the inventor saw the solution of the difficulty, and while he was asking for time he awoke. It was four o'clock in the morning. He jumped out of bed, ran to his workshop, and before nine o'clock he had molded a needle with the eye at the point.

It is not only in the field of mechanics that new processes are developed as the result of dreams. The same creative insight is found in the field of literature also. J. B. Priestly dreamed in complete detail three essays—*The Berkshire Beast, The Strange Outfitter* and *The Dream*. This same process is recognized by Archbishop Temple of Canterbury in his statement, "All decisive thinking goes on behind the scenes; I seldom know when it takes place—much of it certainly during sleep."

The Reverend Henry Ward Beecher, perhaps the outstanding preacher of the last generation, was a busy man and during one period preached every day for eighteen months. His plan was to keep a number of ideas for sermons "incubating." Each night before retiring, Dr. Beecher would select one of these incubating ideas, think intensely about it, then go to sleep. The next morning he would wake with this idea fully developed for a sermon.

In his book, *Across the Plains*, Robert Louis Stevenson has a chapter on dreams, in which he describes his own experiences. By giving a suggestion to his subconscious mind just before falling asleep he was able to obtain vivid dreams which were of great help to him in his literary work. Stevenson credits most of his greatest writing to "the little people who manage man's internal theatre." He recognized that subconscious mental activity came to the surface while he was asleep. He insisted that his "little people" created or fashioned his stories and that this material was imprinted clearly on his waking mind. Stevenson, like most writers, had a period during which his name alone did not assure acceptance of material. It was during this time that he conceived a short story which he titled *The Traveling Companion*, based on the theme of a dual personality—one good, one evil. He completed the story and sent it in to an editor, who promptly rejected it with a note saying, "This is an ingenious piece of work, but your plot is very weak."

Stevenson read the story again and recognized his own inability to improve on the plot. He was inactive for weeks while the unsold story gathered dust instead of dollars. Then he recalled his ability to call forth plots in his dreams, where he would simply stand aside as a spectator and watch the story as it unfolded, without knowing how it would end. Could this extraordinary mental process solve his predicament?

Frustrated and anxious because of his financial situation, before going to sleep one night Stevenson reread the short story previously rejected by his publisher. His subconscious mind became active and in a dream that same night he observed the development of a strange and dramatic plot. He promptly left his bed and recorded it. In the unusual drama which passed through his mind he saw the dual-personality theme of his short story expanded into a plot which brought him fame and furnished to millions of people hours of thrilling suspense, the story of Dr. Jekyll and Mr. Hyde.

Many writers of both poetry and prose, admittedly have been indebted to dreams for their poems and stories. Samuel Taylor Coleridge's "Kubla Khan," that strange unfinished poem which has been described as "unrivaled in the English language for imagery and immaginative suggestion" came to him in a dream. The dream was interrupted while he was writing it and Coleridge never was able to finish the poem.

Many dreams bring to the conscious mind creative wisdom and insight. Luigi Pirandello, the famous Italian winner of the 1934 Nobel Prize in literature, fashioned many of his plays and novels by simply building on his dreams.

Another famous Italian, the poet Bettinelli, made this statement: "The happy moment for the poet may be called a dream, dreamed in the presence of the intellect, which stands by and gazes with open eyes at the performance."

Eileen J. Garrett, a nationally known authority on parapsychology, has an interesting statement along this line:

Dreams in the sleeping state are supposed to be motivated in the subconscious is response to sensory stimuli. But I believe we may add to these the stimuli of purposive intentions in the conscious mind. Such intentions, deposited with the subconscious, have frequently brought me dreams which were ample, if not complete fulfillment of the experience which I sought. One of the most interesting aspects of such experience is the fact that what I sought was usually somebody else's concern, quite impersonal to me, so that the dream material eventually depended for all its value upon the acceptance and understanding of another person. Under such circumstances I have found spread before awareness, on waking, the odd and intimate names of people, places and things, disassociated dates, cryptic phrases and catchwords—absolutely nothing to me. But in reporting these to the person on whose behalf I had sought them, they proved to be coherent and significant to that other consciousness.[4]

In a later section of this study techniques will be described for consciously directing the activity of the subconscious mind. Suggestions will be made regarding the time most auspicious for this purpose. The material presented in this chapter raises several interesting questions. Apparently there is little evidence that subconscious insight can be gained in dreams by consciously asking for this to be done. It is not clear whether the sermons which Dr. Beecher found in his mind each morning were received as a dream, or whether his thinking on a particular subject just previous to retiring had been worked on by the subconscious mind and that its solution was delivered to the conscious mind on his waking. The same question can be raised regarding other instances, particularly Stevenson's use of the subconscious in the production of his literary works.

Apparently subconscious insights gained through dreams come unsolicited or arrive in the presence of an emergency and seem to be an effort of the subconscious to voluntarily assist in the solution of a problem. In most instances subconscious insight delivered by

[4] Eileen J. Garrett, *Awareness* (New York: Farrar, Straus & Cudahy, Inc.). Used by permission.

dreams seems to arrive when the individual has exhausted all possible efforts even to the point of extreme fatigue.

These data regarding subconscious activity as expressed in dreams are evidence of the continuing creative activity of this part of our mind.

6
THE POWER OF THE SUBCONSCIOUS MIND

IN considering the seemingly limitless power exhibited by the subconscious mind, one is reminded of the Heraclitean contention that "Men are Mortal Gods and the Gods Immortal Men." The extraordinary power and goal-achieving wisdom can be illustrated in four aspects:

1. The power and wisdom in directing and sustaining the mysterious processes of the human body.

2. The strange ability of certain individuals to solve mathematical problems.

3. Extraordinary instances of memory recall.

4. Unusual and unbelievable feats of physical strength in times of emergency.

In the whole realm of reality which can be even partially evaluated by intelligence, there is nothing found quite as complex as the processes in the human brain. In this small organ of the human body there are millions and millions of data processing units. Along with these are found a data storage and recall system which is ordinarily called memory. The human brain has perhaps twelve billion nerve cells. A single nerve cell may receive impulses in the same instant from as many as 10,000 others.

The chemical elements of brain cells are simple when extracted in the laboratory. However, the organized processes of these cells are infinitely more complex than the simple chemical elements of which they are made. These cells use electrochemical energy and synthesized proteins and other molecules.

Electricity moves over wires as continuous electromagnetic waves. In a similar way, the signals are transmitted over nerve fibers and are projected from fiber to fiber by what is best described as a chain of electrochemical relay stations.

During mental activity the movement of chemicals across the membrane of an axon is unbelievably rapid—perhaps as many as a thousand movements a second.

The autonomic nerve system has two parts, the sympathetic and the para-sympathetic, which balance each other to secure the proper functioning of body processes. Who or what tells the sympathetic system to speed up the heartbeat in times of excitement or danger? On the other hand, who or what tells the parasympathetic system to slow down the movement of the heart?

The central nervous system of the human body constantly receives a stupendous flow of information impulses or signals—about three billion each minute. Thus the human personality is always receiving a ceaseless electrochemical torrent. Nerve impulses are identical whether we hear music or experience the beauty of a sunset, or move in flight from the presence of danger. Thus, identical impulses of energy produce totally different results. What is it that discriminates and evaluates the meaning of these identical movements of electrochemical energy resulting in all the varied expressions of mental and emotional activity?

No one has ever identified a place where the mind with its thoughts, emotions and consciousness is found. We can observe the operations but we cannot find the location in space of the operator. However complex, and the human brain is indescribably so, this small organ is a strange source—if indeed it is the scource—of dreams, love, intelligence, anger, reason and the values and august intuitions of human personality.

There is only one tenable explanation: The subconscious mind controls and directs all body processes, including those processes by which mental activity and emotional tones are expressed. Only a unit of intelligence with seemingly infinite wisdom is equal to this task.

Consider for a moment nineteen-year-old Shakuntala Devi who can do mathematical problems faster than an electric brain. By the time a veteran mathematician had written the number 24,137,569 on a blackboard, this girl gave the cube root 289, and she found a long list of other roots with equal ease and speed. If we could follow the processes that go on inside the head of this girl, we would certainly learn something interesting about the submerged area of the mind. This girl is one of those calculating wonders that quite frequently appear on the human scene. These strange people are able to perform almost instantaneous mental calculations so fantastic as to seem unbelievable.

Consider Zerah Colburn, an American boy, who went on a tour of Europe at six years of age. At a demonstration in London he raised eight to the sixteenth power (281,474,976,710,656) within one minute. This boy could announce square and cube roots "instantly" and gave, in less than one minute, 641 and 6,700,417 as factors of 4,294,967,207.

An instance of the ability to solve difficult mathematical problems was reported by the *New York Times* (October 26, 1952). David de Klerk Smith, a twenty-seven-year-old bookkeeper of Johannesburg can subtract and multiply at a more rapid rate than figures can be written down. In ten seconds he determined that 2,789 multiplied by 8,362 equaled 23,321,618. In another situation, in fifteen minutes he calculated the number of times a wheel with the diameter of fifteen feet would revolve in fifteen miles. In an equally mystifying display of unusual power, it required only ten seconds for him to multiply forty-seven to the fifth power. A problem which required 142 seconds for a calculating machine to solve, was accomplished by him in thirty-nine seconds.

Early in the Eighteenth Century a youngster by the name of George Biddle became a challenge and a mystery to the intellectual circles of Great Britain. This boy was the son of a poverty-stricken stonecutter and showed his unusual ability at the age of six. His father sent him to Edinburgh University where he won a prize for unusual mathematical work. When George was twelve years old, a group of educators asked him to find the answer to this problem: If a pendulum swings nine and three-quarter inches in one second, how many inches will it swing in seven years, fourteen days, two hours, one minute and fifty-six seconds—counting each year as 365 days, five hours, forty minutes and fifty seconds? In less than one minute's time the genius of George Biddle provided the answer— 2,165,625,744¾ inches.

George Biddle grew to manhood and became one of the world's greatest civil engineers. His construction of Victoria Docks stands as a monument to his unusual ability.

Instances of this type of unusual and extraordinary mathematical power, present without training or special instruction, have been found in literally hundreds of such people. Strangely enough with maturity or training this power ordinarily, but not always, declines.

In the field of music and art, examples are found of extraordinary power in the very young. When he was three years old, Mozart played the piano. He completed his first opera by the time he was twelve. Franz Lizst started playing the piano when only six years of age and held concerts from his eighth year on. Schubert wrote sonatas, symphonies and operas when he was only eleven and twelve years of age. Before he was twelve, K. M. Weber had written six symphonies, three sonatas and an opera.

Examples of this same power are found in other areas. Raphael began drawing at age eight. Some of his work was accepted at the Academy in Venice when he was only twelve. At eighteen he was already famous. Dante composed his "Sonnet to Beatrice" when he was only nine. Victor Hugo had to his credit over 3,000 verses by the time he was eleven years old. Frederich Gauss worked mathematical problems and traced geometrical figures in the dust when only a small child three years of age. He later became one of the great authorities in the field of mathematics.

Perhaps one of the most incredible cases of memory recall is that of Tom Wiggins. He was an imbecile child born on the plantation of a family in Alabama in the year 1840. His mother, a slave girl servant in the plantation home, kept the child near in the "big house" so that she might protect him from injury through his blind groping.

Tom was about six years old when, one night, the family entertained. The daughter and her mother-in-law, both accomplished musicians, played for their guests, the elder lady rendering a new and quite difficult selection. After the departure of the guests that evening, the family retired as usual. The daughter of the plantation owner had slept but a short time when she was awakened by sounds from the piano in the library. Continuing to listen she heard her mother-in-law's musical rendition being repeated in the lady's characteristic manner. She arose and went to the library door. At the piano sat little Tom Wiggins, his fingers flying over the keys with the skill of a professional. The boy had crawled through the open window and reached the piano in some manner which was difficult to understand.

An amazing prodigy had come to light. Tom's sole gift was imitation. Following a musician, who had missed a note, the blind musician would make the same error. No matter whether he had ever heard a piece of music before, little Tom could go to the piano and follow the performer with a complete rendition of the selection, not omitting any feature of expression.

Tom and his gift were exhibited at first in the southern cities and towns. Then, as the boy's fame spread over the country, he played to audiences in practically every city in the nation during the next twenty-five years, as well as in many of the chief cities of Europe. He played for many crowned heads, and some of the world's greatest composers, none of whom could find any explanation of the phenomenon. How he ever acquired knowledge and skill, the relative position of the keys, and their accompanying sounds when struck, remains a mystery.

It will be recalled that Toscanini had a phenomenal ability to recall. While conducting, he never used notes of any kind. On a typical occasion, he led the orchestra and singers through the four acts of *La Boheme* without a note in front of him.

That the subconscious mind is always active in the normal affairs of life is illustrated by an incident in the life of Henry Clay. This happened during Clay's older years and at a time when he was unable to reply at length on the floor of the Senate to an opponent who had made an address of vital interest to Clay. He decided to speak but fearful that he would overtax his strength, he asked a friend sitting nearby to stop him by fair means or foul at the end of ten minutes.

The friend nudged Clay at the agreed moment but he kept right on with the speech; the hint was repeated none too gently and again ignored. A pin was brought into play but Clay's subconscious mind, with its array of facts and logic was thoroughly aroused. Feeling that he "must say something," he continued in one of the most eloquent efforts of his life for more than two hours. In his exhaustion at the close of his speech he reproached his friend severely for permitting him to exceed the ten minutes since that was the length of the speech which he had consciously prepared. Afterwards he stated to his friends that records of facts, which normally he had forgotten, trooped and marched through his mind, that he felt no nudge and no pin during the time.

The power of the subconscious mind to act on a suggestion is illustrated by an extraordinary event that occurred in one of the European nations. Physicians had been given permission to experiment on a criminal who had been sentenced to death. The prisoner was told that he was to bleed to death. He was placed on a table, his eyes covered and then small incisions made on his arm but not deep enough to cause blood to flow. A small stream of running water was allowed to trickle down over his arm into a bowl and this he felt and heard distinctly. Standing by, the attending physicians were making remarks on the progress of the bleeding and his growing weakness and approaching death. In a short time the prisoner died and he had all the symptoms of cariac syncope from the loss of blood.

Subconscious energy, when properly directed by suggestions, has the power not only to kill but also to build up and restore health. In my home town there was the case of a man who was ill and in the crisis point of the disease. From the standpoint of medical science he had not one chance in a hundred of recovering. Much depended upon the ability and willingness of the patient to set in motion his own will—his will to survive.

By arrangement with physicians and nurses, the patient was able to hear their apparently secret conference in which they stated that at that time he was past all danger, that he had gone through the crisis safely but that this must not be discussed with him. Had he been told directly that he was all right he would have suspected the purpose of the physician but when he heard them endeavoring to keep their remarks from him, his eagerness to hear made the comments more than distinct. From that moment he took on new power. To the surprise of everyone, he recovered.

The dramatic power of subconscious action is perhaps best illustrated by emergency situations. The conscious mind knows that it must operate with limited power in a restricted field. The subconscious accepts no such limitation. Apparently the subconscious has potentially at its command unlimited power. This potentially unlimited power is restricted only by the assumptions of the conscious mind. In emergency situations the conscious mind is thrust aside, permitting the wisdom and power of subconscious action to express itself.

It is well known that sudden fright or danger will release every particle of energy and enable a paralytic or cripple to perform unusual feats of strength. Some years ago a Los Angeles newspaper published a story telling how "Frances Avita, frail and weighing only 100 pounds, lifted a heavy automobile off the head of her brother and saved his life after an auto accident. Summoning superhuman strength, the girl was able to lift over 900 pounds, a weight which no ordinary man could move."

A member of the Lewis and Clark Expedition was captured by hostile Indians. His clothing was removed and he was told he could run for his life. This was a form of exquisite torture in the minds of the Indians who prided themselves on being such rapid runners that they could quickly overtake any white man. What these Indians did not consider was the superhuman strength which the glands of internal secretion makes available when the human personality is experiencing intense fear.

The young man was able to keep ahead long enough to reach a sharp walled depression several hundred feet deep. Without stopping to consider the difficulty, the young man leaped across it. The Indians, not inspired by fear, were unable to accomplish this. At a later time this young man returned to this scene and almost fainted when he saw the distance which he had jumped.

What gives a lone, frail woman the strength to lift an automobile and release her brother whose life is in danger?

From what source does the soldier in battle receive strength to perform amazing acts of heroism and daring?

What energy or force empowered the *suggestion that a man was to bleed to death, to cause him to die?*

It is through the subconscious mind that seemingly unlimited power and strength are available in such times of emergency and danger.

During World War I, I was stationed in a large hospital in central France. The impression of a certain patient, suffering from shock but without physical injury, remains vividly in mind. This person remained for a number of days in an upright position on his cot with his right arm extended straight out in front of his shoulder. No support was given and nothing could induce or enable him to change the position of his arm. As every physician knows, it would be utterly impossible for a person to sustain his arm in such a position through the normal action of his mind and body for a few hours, much less several days. From what source, then, came the energy for this action? Certainly not from the conscious self.

Literally hundreds of similar experiences are known to science. In the presence of danger, superhuman strength is available. What is the source of this vast reserve of power? What stimulus or mental or emotional channel brings it to the surface? Such extraordinary power, such limitless and immediate wisdom must find (insofar as present-day knowledge is concerned) its source in the largely unexplored field of subconscious motivation.

7

THE
GOAL-DIRECTED LIFE

OVER the entrance to the Temple of Apollo at Delphi was placed the statement, "Know Thyself." The ancient priests of Apollo described in this statement the process or law by which all success is attained and through which all happiness and satisfaction come to the individual.

This law of success involves just two things—you, and what and how you think. You are now just what, and only what, you desire to be. By every thought and every feeling growing out of your mind, you have built the house in which you now live. Whether the house is large or small, rich or poor; whether you are successful or crushed down by failure—you and you alone are responsible.

The ancient Greek fable of Pygmalion and Galatea is an interesting story. Pygmalion, the bachelor god, because of his distrust and dislike of women in general, decided to create his own ideal companion. Being a sculptor, he chiseled a female statue with great skill and infinite patience, from the finest ivory. So beautiful was the figure that no woman could be found that equaled in any way the grace of form and exquisite charm embodied in Pygmalion's statue. Indeed, his work was of such perfection that it seemed to be alive and was prevented from moving about only by a maidenly sense of modesty. Many of those who passed the studios of this bachelor god, looking upon the beautiful form, forgot that it was the work of Pygmalion's hand and not a creation of Nature at her best.

Pygmalion, too, admired the statue and finally fell in love with it. He arrayed the statue in gowns of rare beauty and put a ring on its finger and a necklace about its neck. His devotion grew and, finally, in his heart he called the ivory virgin his wife.

The festival of Venus was at hand—a festival celebrated with great pomp and solemn beauty. Victims were offered, smoke rose from the altar, and the odor of incense filled the air. When Pygmalion, the bachelor god, performed his devotion, he stood before the altar and timidly said, "Oh, great gods who can do all things, give me I pray you for my wife"—he dared not say—"my ivory virgin," but said instead, "one like my ivory virgin." The goddess Venus being present and knowing the inner thoughts of Pygmalion, as a token of her favor, caused the flame on the altar to rise up high three times into the air.

When Pygmalion returned home from the festival of devotion and approached the ivory statue, she seemed more lovely than ever. Timidly and with great reverence, he placed a kiss upon her lips. With joy, Pygmalion observed movements of the statue's arms. As he stood, filled with wonder and joy, the virgin statue became alive, embodying all the grace and charm and beauty which he had visioned as he carved the statue from the block of ivory. Pygmalion created his own destiny by mental and emotional activity within himself.

The concept of achievement, of plenty, of success, held steadfastly in mind and empowered by strong emotional impulses, will bring the experience of abundance. On the other hand, let fear and worry be your mental companions, let thoughts of poverty and limitations dwell in your mind, and as surely as the night follows the day, worry, fear, limitations and poverty will be expressed in your experience. Mental and emotional activity will supply you with limitless energy and will take whatever form your mind demands. Thoughts are the molds which form this energy into good or ill, success or failure, according to the idea you impress upon it. It is not only that every person is free to select positive or negative thoughts, but by the very nature of life, everyone must do just this.

Mind creates by making things out of itself by activity within itself. To bring you what you need or want, mind acts within itself upon itself. In each and every condition, whether of great fortune or failure, you and you alone are responsible. By thought and feeling, we create our own destiny.

The first principle of success is an urgent, insistent desire, a feeling of lack, a feeling of need for something that you do not have.

Desire is the planting of the seed of achievement. Desire comes from within, from the very center of life. No seed ever germinated and expressed itself in the form of plant or tree except by processes from within. Desire, the thing or condition that a person wants, determines the way that life will go, not only its direction but its attainment.

Some while ago I visited the family home of Helen Keller at Tuscumbia, Alabama. Standing under the great oaks that tower above this modest home, peaceful and quiet in the early evening hour, it was difficult to recapture anything of the great drama of struggle and achievement which attended the unfolding of this most unusual of women. The story of the afflictions of Helen Keller is known around the world. The story of her achievement in overcoming these limitations forms an epic which children and adults alike will read as long as romance and drama appeal to the human heart. Deaf, dumb and blind, she was cut off completely from all the avenues by which a person's life is expressed. Something within Helen Keller was stronger than physical limitations. Her rebellion was complete and thoroughgoing. Even as a small child she refused to accept her condition. Her imprisoned spirit demanded contact with the normal things of life. No medical skill on earth could give this to Helen Keller. Neither love nor riches were of any avail. The spirit within was stronger than the limitations imposed from without. Even fate itself could not imprison Helen Keller. She would not accept it.

Every normal person desires four things:

First, bodily strength, vitality, exuberant, youthful health and vigor.

Second, an abudance of things and services, a good salary, a reasonable reserve of money or property—in a word, security.

Third, the security and happiness made possible and found only in an intelligent, just, social order—brotherhood, democracy.

Fourth, contact with Infinite Power, the assurance that life has ultimate meaning and purpose. You want to believe that social and spiritual values achieved through eons of struggle and suffering will be conserved.

If there is sanity in the Universe, then these things are the birthright of every individual.

When the War Between the States freed the slaves, one young Negro took his bride and went into the hills of Alabama to start a new life. Against all custom he had, in slavery days, taught himself to read and write. Of the twelve children of this couple, one is the father of a remarkable family of six today, all born in Montgomery. These six, between them, have fourteen academic degrees, including several from Harvard and Columbia and one from Vienna. One of these six is Dr. Percy L. Julian, head of the Soya Bean Products Laboratories at the Glidden Company's plant in Chicago.

In Percy's youth there was no high school for his race in Montgomery. One day he climbed the fence around the white high school and watched intently the boys at work in the chemical laboratory. A policeman pulled him down and sent him off packing to his mother. His mother comforted him and promised him that he would one day be a chemist. And this is what he became.

He worked with tutors and finally went to a mission school. He and his brothers and sisters worked as newsboys, bellhops, busboys, nursemaids. His father worked as a mail clerk and went without lunches; his mother took in washings. One steady flame lighted that humble home: ambition—ambition for an education. DePauw University at Greencastle, Indiana, was chosen because it welcomed all races. When he graduated, he was valedictorian and Phi Beta Kappa orator. He won his M.A. at Harvard and his Ph.D. at the University of Vienna.

Some years ago in Chicago more than 700 top citizens gathered at the Morrison Hotel to pay honor to the "Chicagoan of the Year," the person who, by his personal accomplishments during 1949, did most for the city. They honored the man who synthesized cortisone and other drugs which promise so much in the fight against arthritis and rheumatic fever. They honored Dr. Percy Julian.

All five of his brothers and sisters have made distinguished names for themselves in science and education. None of the six waited for "breaks." Against the most formidable obstacles they made their own opportunities. They have brought added luster and fame to Alabama and the nation.

It is true that failures and disappointments belong to the changing fortunes of every man and woman. No one can escape their dangerous whirlpools forever. Those who do escape from one failure and swim on to safety are the ones who accept and trust temporary defeats as inevitable experiences faced on the path of success. They ride them through and reach their goal. Elbert Hubbard reminded us: "A failure is a man who has blundered, but is not able to cash in on his experience."

The difference is that between the two frogs in Dr. Alfred Adler's well-know story. The frogs fell into a tall pail of fresh milk. The one, beholding his dangerous plight, began moaning piteously, "I'm going to drown. I'm going to drown. I'm going to drown." His body sagged and his legs feebly pawed the surface of the milk. Within a few moments he went down. The other furiously paddled with his legs, shouting, "I've got to get out. I've got to get out." Soon he found himself standing on a cake of butter he had churned. He jumped out to safety. If, like Adler's frogs, you find yourself in a bad situation, don't whine and sink. Keep on kicking. You can overcome anything if you invest your full strength.

Among the wise men of India there is a legend that "when God was equipping man for his life-journey of exploration, the attending

angel was about to add the gift of contentment and complete satisfaction. The Infinite Mind stayed his hand. "No," He said, "if you
give him that power you will rob him forever of the joy of self-
discovery." Find and use the resources and powers within you.

One of the basic ingredients for directing one's life successfully
is an open-minded willingness to consider new facts. Simply because a thing has never been done is not a reason for assuming
that it can never be done. The story of each human advance is that
of some bold, courageous mind meeting the resistance of the status
quo—the idea that simply because a thing has never been done, it
cannot and should not be accomplished.

Experts are frequently wrong as to the practical value and worth
of new ideas. Trained professional men are very often conservative,
so completely that they are unwilling to look at new facts. When
Harvey discovered the circulation of the blood, he was criticized,
rejected, called a charlatan and anti-Christ simply because he had
gained new understanding regarding the human body.

During all the centuries of human history men have dreamed of
flying. Practical men were always skeptical that it could be done.
The German philosopher and mathematician, von Leibnitz, said
regarding efforts to create a heavier-than-air flying machine, "Here
God has, so to speak, put a bar against man's path." The French
astronomer, Lalande, demonstrated with apparently irresistible
facts and arguments that flying was a scientific impossibility. When
the Wright brothers made their first successful demonstration at
Kitty Hawk, a reporter wired his New York newspaper an account
of the demonstration. So utterly skeptical and unbelieving was the
editor that he not only did not publish the story but made the reporter pay for the telegram.

Some of us ride in comfort on trains today. When locomotives
first reached the speed of thirty miles an hour, The Munich College
of Physicians issued an earnest warning against railway travel.
They feared that trees and houses flashing past the eyes would
damage vision and the dizzy speed would bring on headaches and
vertigo. In wise old England it was predicted that traveling at
thirty miles an hour would cause insanity.

When Alexander Graham Bell began his experiments with the telephone in 1874 the professional engineers all said, "This is the triumph of folly." Practical men who were his contemporaries saw Bell not as a genius but a troublesome youngster who neglected his duties to follow an impossible idea.

Jenner's vaccination for smallpox, Semmeleweis' contribution to the prevention of childbed fever and Findlay's discovery of the role played by the mosquito in transmitting yellow fever, followed long, discouraging trial-and-error experiments during which authorities believe the innovator to be following a blind alley.

There is just one blind alley in the Universe and that is a closed mind. Intellectual curiosity, a willingness to consider and evaluate all facts, whatever their source, is a basic element in a goal-directed life. Did you ever hear of Tantalus? Perhaps there never was such a person, but he appears in an old legend that carries meaningful insight for everyone. Tantalus had offended the gods, so he was doomed to live in water up to his chin but could never drink the water even though he was tortured with thirst.

In the same way many people live miserably, never having enough, always trying to reach their goals and always failing—this for the simple reason, in many cases, that the mind is closed to new facts and to new approaches to problems.

From another standpoint the question becomes: What kind of a person do you see when you look at yourself? At the very center of personality there is always found an image of the self. This self-image is the result of your mental and emotional processes as determined by your conscious and subconscious mind. The self-image may not be visible to other people, but it always exists at the center of your personality. It is what you feel and recognize yourself to be.

Your present situation, be it one of prosperity or poverty, of sickness or health, of self-confidence and social acceptance, or frustration and failure, is an exact reflection of your self-image. You must think only what you wish to experience and become.

It is basic to remember that you created this self-image. It may have been influenced by heredity or environmental conditions, but your self-image is more than the sum total of these. It is the inner reality of your life which you have created. Whatever this self-image may be, you are responsible. You did the building.

Modern man has to a large degree lost his sense of purpose, his feeling of integrity and self-control. The feeling has developed that the individual is but a hapless pawn at the mercy of relentless and purposeless cosmic forces. An interesting sidelight on the modern scene is that of scientists (and a far greater number not wearing this accolade) who are motivated by the continuing purpose of proving that they and the Universe are purposeless.

To form a self-image that will permit a full development of personality, faith must be recaptured in the age-long aspiration of humanity, that the Universe is a living purposeful exhibition of an Inscrutable Mind. Perhaps the simplest and at the same time the most profound statement of this philosophy ever made is found in one of Tennyson's poems—"Nothing Walks with Aimless Feet."

Goal-directed action is present in all physical processes of our bodies. The great medical scientist, Alexis Carrel, tells the dramatic story of small drops of blood building a blood tube apparently out of nothing. It is the nature of blood to run through tubes. However, blood is nothing but blood; while blood tubes are composed of membrane cells, muscle cells, fiber, and connective tissue cells. Blood cells do not contain a single trace of any cell of which blood tubes are built, yet these blood cells have creative power and in some strange way bring into being the various kinds of cells needed. This action of blood cells illustrates the process of life making things out of itself, within itself for a selected purpose of self-expression.

Self-directed, creative action is found in the basic unit of all life. Consider the amoeba which carries on the tradition of a remote past. The amoeba has no stomach, yet it eats and digests food. Having neither gills nor lungs, yet it breathes. Without fins, wings, or legs, it travels. The amoeba is utterly without brains, yet it makes a good living. Perhaps strangest of all, without a reproductive system, this organism breeds effectively and more rapidly than any other creature. With a body invisible to the naked eye, it does almost everything a dinosaur of forty tons could do. In fact, this microscopic unit of life has resources and wisdom which have kept its name on the roll for all the uncounted centuries since the evolutionary process began on this planet.

Nothing in the world is left to chance or luck. Every action—all forms of behavior—are caused. All activity—whether we realize it or not—is goal-seeking. Each one of us by the very nature of the life process, selects the goal or objective we want to achieve.

Life can be managed. It can be directed toward a chosen objective. You need not be a puppet moved by strings held by an unseen hand.

The first ingredient must be recognition of the innate greatness and power within your mind. The late Lecomte du Nou'y said that it required 1,600,000,000 years to evolve the human mind. Regardless of its ancestral development, mind is the measuring rod of reality. In fact, mind is the only reality in a world of vanishing matter. You are mind. The force behind all progress and achievement is energy applied by mind. Correctly used, your mind will bring you whatever you want or need.

Keep in mind that life is a struggle between two basic drives. All of us know the urge to live. The instinct of self-preservation is back of almost everything we plan and do. We should also remember that the opposite of this constructive impulse, self-destruction, is a part of our equipment. Dr. Peter J. Steincrohn has said, "It is a proven insight of psychiatry and psychology that the 'death instinct' is implanted in the very structure of personality." Whatever the explanation may be, it is a fact of experience that some people prefer death to life, illness to health, and failure to success.

Dorothea Brande has a very stimulating discussion of the will to fail: "Absurd as it may seem at first consideration, that anyone would solemnly enter into even an unconscious conspiracy to fail, it is a matter of observation that there is hardly one person in a hundred who does not, in some fashion, deliberately cripple and thwart himself. . . . With the time and energy we spend in making failure a certainty, we might have certain success." [1]

[1] Dorothea Brande, *Wake Up and Live* (New York: Simon and Schuster, Inc.). Used by permission.

This will to fail can be overcome and expelled by giving the sub-conscious the nutrients of the will to succeed. Don't short-circuit your plans by self-pity, fear and routine thinking. Your will—the will to succeed—is supreme, if it is sustained and supported by purposely-directed subconscious power.

The assumption made by this study is that human experience is a training ground, the purpose of which is to develop and expand the latent power of the human personality. Life is neither a rose garden nor a rubbish dump. For the individual person, life is intended to be a school of experience in which the creative energy potential implanted by the Source of Life is developed and trained for increasing responsibilities.

Perhaps the greatest mistake of our day is our failure to understand the ability of the adult mind to recreate and redirect itself. This ability confirms the wisdom expressed by a great English jurist when he said, "You hold the key within yourself with which to unlock the secret chamber that contains your heart's desire."

If we are to experience a goal-directed life, we must have two things: faith and work.

We must believe there's a point to our labors. If tomorrow science should show us proof that this earth is a clay ball flying aimlessly through meaningless space, and inhabited by creatures with no pattern and no purpose, it would be necessary for us to reject it and somehow build a world and a Universe in the depths of our personality in which we could believe.

We must work. We must do the job we set for ourselves. This means the acceptance of a personal duty; and when that duty is accepted, it becomes the paid-up ticket of a self-directed citizen. We have to believe this is a world in which progress can be achieved, one brick and stone upon another. And we must accept the fact that each of us must lay his share of those bricks and stones.

There isn't any escalator service to success and achievement . . . or to heaven.

8

PREPARATION, IMAGINATION AND VISUALIZATION

IN the literature on mental activity the statement is frequently made that the subconscious mind is all powerful, that it has infinite wisdom and that it can accomplish anything an individual wants to achieve. It is perfectly true that we do not know the limits of the wisdom and power of this aspect of personality. Certainly the subconscious mind is a source of energy with superior wisdom and creative ability; however, it does not partake of the nature of Aladdin's lamp. It is a part of the makeup of every individual, but what it achieves and what it can do depends upon how it is used by the conscious mind.

Recall the statement previously made ·that the conscious mind is the self-knowing activity of a person. It is self-starting and, therefore, self-directing. The conscious mind can decide what it wants to think, what it wants to achieve and how it will respond to the action of other minds. Also recall the fact that the subconscious mind is the obedient servant of the self-aware conscious mind. It receives, retains and works upon that which is given into it by the self-knowing conscious mind.

The first thing to do is to recognize and consciously accept the fact that you are conscious and subconscious mind. The subconscious aspect of mind is present at birth and remains an inseparable part of your life whether or not you recognize this fact. This activity of the subconscious mind is inescapable. In a very real sense, this submerged mental and emotional activity has made you what you are today. It will inexorably continue to function whether you ever give it a thought or not. The important thing to remember is that this underlying energy of mind can be directed, that it can be controlled, that it will sustain and tend to bring into actualization whatever you desire. The oft repeated statement—Whatever mind can conceive, it can achieve, is true only if the mental conception is competent and adequate for the goal visualized.

To successfully direct and use subconscious energy requires sustained and consistent effort. It is true that activity by this part of the mind will relieve your workload and will enhance your ability, but this will only be accomplished if you consciously, purposefully and systematically direct and control its processes.

If you are serious about this business of improving your mental activity, the first thing to recognize is that the subconscious aspect of mind will not and cannot relieve you of the necessity for study and preparation, neither will it remove the need for clear, consistent, rational thinking. If you have a problem to solve, the first thing to do is to study and bring into the focus of your conscious mind every fact accessible to you relating to this problem.

Before any major problem is given to the subconscious to work on, the known facts and related data should be assembled and examined from every angle until it is understood. The arguments for and against any particular solution should be worked out in detail. After all the facts are gathered, the problem or question should be stated in specific terms, preferably on paper. In a word, the subconscious mind should be given a specification. But this caution should be observed: The specification should involve the result, not the method. Often the subconscious mind attacks a problem from an oblique angle and we do not realize at the time that it has solved it. We are so used to thinking on the basis of conventional approaches that we often overlook what seems unpromising, perhaps even foolish—but may turn out to be the obvious solution. And it is the obvious that we are forever overlooking.

Unless your desire for a solution is sufficiently intense for you to investigate all aspects of the matter, unless you consistently correlate and interpret every element in the situation to the best of your ability, you will find that subconscious insight will be incomplete and inadequate. It is trite but true that the most difficult task the average person faces is to center his mind upon any group of facts for an extended period of time. Superficial, unrealistic and hasty thinking will be faithfully reflected back to your conscious mind by your sustaining subconscious activity.

If you are not seeking the solution of an immediate, well-defined problem, but simply desire to use your subconscious mind to develop a more integrated, mature outlook on life, the same law of mind prevails. A mature viewpoint is the result of understanding. Understanding arrives because basic background material has been considered. It is not enough to express the following verbally and intermittently:

"All things work together for good,"
"I will achieve my objective,"
"My life is successful and prosperous."

Such statements simply verbalized and temporarily held in the conscious mind, of course, have limited value. Mental and emotional activity is a continuous process; only when constructive ideas are directed to the subconscious mind can we build healthy bodies, harmonius emotions and creative, radiant mentality.

Library shelves contain many books on "positive thinking"—on the effect of mental and emotional processes upon physical and mental health; in fact, the literature covers the whole range of personality building and function. To plant this idea of maturity, balance and poise in your subconscious mind, you need to reinforce your affirmations and assumptions by reading and absorbing some of the many useful books written for this purpose. If you are concerned with a philosophy of life, the higher values to be obtained by human experience, your place and function in the Universe, then give your subconscious mind the inspiration found in the thinking of men and women who have attained eminence in this field. When this is done you will find that the very structure of your personality is rebuilt and that you will embody within yourself a new dynamic for living.

Assume that you face a problem and desire to find a solution. Assume further that you have investigated and gathered all available facts bearing on the question at hand and that you have also considered in a rational, common-sense way everything about the problem and have not arrived at a satisfactory conclusion. In such a situation, turn the whole matter over to your subconscious mind. The best time to do this is just before going to sleep at night. After you have retired, let the main stream of facts hurriedly pass before your mind and acknowledge that you do not have a solution to the problem. At this point, in a calm, purposeful voice state your need to find a solution. Clothe your statement with understanding of the function and nature of the subconscious, empowered by expectancy and confidence. Your verbal statement should be repeated several times. At this time turn the whole matter over to your subconscious and go to sleep.

The subconscious mind never sleeps—it is always awake and under all conditions active. During sleep the conscious part of your mind is inactive. It stands relaxed, aside from the problems of the day. This removes the inhibitions, negative ideas and mistaken concepts held by the conscious mind. The underlying part of your mind is then free to develop its synthesis and to do its creative work.

A study of the great inventions, important insights in psychology and medicine, in all branches of science, in music and art, show that the period immediately following sleep in the early morning is more often than not the time during which subconscious wisdom arrives in the conscious mind. This period when you are just emerging from deep sleep into something like a light trance or reverie is very important. At times when a solution is desired from the subconscious, it is important that you remain quiet, relaxed and without conscious mental activity for a short period of time after you are awake. The whole history of human thought indicates that this is a fertile moment during which to receive the insight and guidance of subconscious mentation.

This matter of mental, emotional and physical relaxation at stated periods is highly important. Subconscious insight has a way of emerging in a very unorthodox fashion. Numerous thoughtful people report that they receive solutions to problems only during periods of relaxation and frequently during periods when the mind is in a general way concerned with other matters. The early morning hours of the day, especially during the period for bathing and dressing, have been the time when new and significant insight and knowledge have emerged from the subconscious. Driving an automobile while mentally and emotionally relaxed is frequently a time of reception for new ideas.

It is well established that subconscious directions seldom, if ever, come when the individual is consciously working on the problem. In some strange way, conscious mental activity closes the door through which the new insight must come.

The image-making ability of the conscious mind is an important key to the direction and control of subconscious activity. It was one of the wisest men this world has ever produced, Marcus Aurelius, who long ago said, "A man's life is dyed by the color of his imagination." In our own day, Albert Einstein has stated, "Imagination is more important than knowledge." Franz Hartmann correctly stated, "The first power that meets us at the threshold of the soul's domain is the power of imagination." That mystic and literary genius, William Blake, stated, "The imagination, the real and eternal world of which this Universe is but a faint shadow . . ."

Shakespeare was not only a great writer but he also had a deep understanding of the working of the human mind. The following statement is evidence of his deep understanding, as well as the creative power of man's image-making faculty:

". . . as imagination bodies forth
The forms of things unknown, the poet's pen
Turns them to shapes and gives to airy nothings
A local habitation and a name."

In a recent study published following his death, Harold Rugg, one of the most distinguished educational pioneers of our time, explores in a challenging way the creative activity of mind. Rugg speaks of new insight as an "imagined conception." He feels that the area of creative work occurs in the consciousness continuum at a point between the conscious mind and what he terms the "non-conscious." This area of mind he describes as the "transliminal mind."

In speaking of the role of imagination in the creative process, Rugg says, "Imagination is the instrument of discovery. The poet and the scientist agree. Discovery is conceiving in imagination, or more succinctly, discovery is imagined conception. . . . Imagination is the universal and indispensable instrument of all levels of living in the human world. Our daily lives are dependent upon it." [1]

It was an act of prepared imagination that enabled Newton to move from the idea of a falling apple to a falling moon. The fertile imagination of Dalton formed the atomic theory out of the data of chemistry. The discoveries of Faraday resulted from his richly endowed imaginative faculty. In short, the process of creative thought is imaginative visioning.

Our thinking is limited and restricted when we are conscious of our thinking process. Intellectual and imaginative creation is accomplished by subconscious mentation. Wordsworth refers to the imagination as, "That intellectual lens through the medium of which the poetical observer sees the objects of his observation modified both in form and color."

Imaginative vision produces a multitude of impressions on the subconscious. Imagination gives motion and vitality to the thought or the idea. In this process the idea is developed into a moving picture acted out in the presence of the subconscious in a series of scenes, visions or pictures, all of them alive and active. Thus the idea becomes a living force in the mind, actually doing the thing, playing the part and living out the basic idea or concept. The mind acting out an idea or concept in this way, produces a series of im-

[1] Harold Rugg, *Imagination* (New York: Harper & Row, Publishers). Used by permission.

pressions instead of just one or a few as is usually the case when autosuggestions are being made to the subconscious.

The keynote for successful image-making is this: Create in your conscious mind the image of things, or conditions, as you would have them to be instead of as they are. Close your eyes and make clear mental pictures sustained by strong emotions. Daydream but daydream with a purpose. This process has creative power. Its basic foundation is found in Plato's axiom, "We become what we contemplate." In this image-building process, it must be remembered that the subconscious mind is not merely a passive realm of engrams or memory patterns, but a very active area of mental and emotional life. This aspect of mind is dynamic and creative.

It is known that in creative activity in literature, music and science, imaginative visioning has frequently been used. Beethoven stated that he always had some picture in his mind when composing. Clerk Maxwell made it a habit to construct a mental picture of every problem. Charles Dickens reported that he saw his stories and then wrote them down. During his career, Thackeray made notes in his books, not only in writing, but also with brush and pencil.

You can use the process of imaginative visioning to plant in your subconscious mind the picture of what you want to achieve. Your subconscious mind reacts immediately to what you think or imagine to be true. It is certainly evident that any person's experience at any time is a direct reflection of that person's thinking habits. The sage of New England, Emerson, truly said, "What we are, that only can we see."

Use your image-making faculty to impress your subconscious mind, to create a visual concept or blueprint of the condition or thing you want. Since the subconscious works from the general to the particular, a mental picture will effectively plant your conception in this part of your mind. It is important to remember that the subconscious does not know the difference between an image or a picture you hold in your mind and a picture which you see hanging on the wall of your study or work room. This means that this part of the mind does not recognize the difference between that which you hold in your conscious mind, empowered by strong desire and expectancy, and an actual occurrence. The subconscious is impressed by thoughts and emotions—not by things.

To create a visual concept of a condition or change that will influence the subconscious, the picture or image must be held in the mind in vivid and complete detail. The subconscious will work only on that which the conscious mind sees. The visual image must correspond to the architect's complete drawing and not simply the artist's picture of the outline of the building. More directly stated, all the facts must be considered.

This process of visualization also applies when the purpose is simply to create a new self-image. The subconscious is not only a source of power for intellectual activity but it is also the fountain out of which our emotions or feelings emerge. The subconscious will empower an emotion expressing hatred or resentment just as readily as it will build normal, healthy attitudes. In fact, much of our tendency toward negative or unfriendly thinking is due to a "feedback" from previous unfavorable experience. A reserve of strength for creative accomplishment is built into your personality only by your subconscious thinking and feeling.

In the next chapter the role of autosuggestion in giving direction for subconscious activity will be explored briefly. It should also be recognized that suggestions enter the subconscious from various sources.

The influence of hetero-suggestions (suggestions or thoughts received from people, from information gained from reading and from occurrences which you witness) is rarely given sufficient consideration. Some persons are inclined to seek advice from every Tom, Dick and Sally before making a decision. These people, much the same as a sponge, soak up all the doubts, misgivings, fears and trepidations experienced by others. The person who successfully manages his mind must recognize his own responsibility for courageous, rational thinking and evaluation. It is good to seek the advice of qualified people, but the final responsibility rests upon you. If you, like a mirror, simply reflect the doubts and negative thinking of other persons you are, to the extent that this is true, planting in your subconscious mind conflicts and negative attitudes which will prevent creative subconscious activity.

In planning to manage your mind and emotions it is usually a mistake to take others into your confidence. Due to unfavorable experience and limited training, the great majority of people make a negative approach to any problem. Tough-minded objective thinking is seldom found. In making your plans, consider all aspects of the problem, form your decision and keep that decision within your own mind.

9
AUTOSUGGESTION

IF the subconscious is to be the servant of the conscious mind, it is important to know how it can be reached and by what method direction and information can be given to it. It is only in the conscious part of the mind that the power of choice or the ability to select is found. Furthermore, since the subconscious mind does not discriminate, does not decide what is good and what is bad, its selecting and deciding must be done for it by the conscious mind. It is not intelligent in the sense that it can select or reject what is given to it, so it must be directed with care.

The subconscious is reached, first of all, by what we generally term "autosuggestion." By this term only one thing is meant; talking to one's self. Since the subconscious is a part of the person, the person is certainly talking to himself when he talks to his subconscious. Conscious mind can control the creative power of the subconscious only by direction—by autosuggestion. The technique of autosuggestion is simply "the subconscious realization of an idea which tends to transfer itself into action." It is based on the principle that what you tell yourself repeatedly with confidence and expenctancy you will eventually believe and that this belief will be realized in your experience.

Our subconscious mind will believe anything and everything

we say to it. That is why the statement made popular by the great French psychiatrist, Coué, "Every day in every way I am getting better and better," was sound psychology. The all-inclusive thought that life progresses, enhanced in meaning and value, when directed repeatedly to the subconscious, will convince that area of the mind that the statement is true; and what is more important, that the statement embodies what the conscious mind really wants to be true.

When told this, the subconscious mind applies all its power toward creating a more wholesome, efficient type of living, drawing on its stored knowledge and experience. Every day in every way one actually becomes better and better.

That this method, as used by Coué, did actually cure thousands of sick people was a fact. That it improved the lives of other thousands who were not sick, but who wanted to live still happier and healthier lives, is equally true.

The role of autosuggestion in everyday life is far greater than is ordinarily believed. In medical fields its dynamic influence is understood. One of the oldest items in the physician's "bag of tricks" is the placebo. It may be a pill or an injection, but however it is served up, the formula is usually the same, a massive dose of pure suggestion mixed with some innocuous substance. Although placebos have been used frequently to establish controlled groups in medical investigations, only limited research has been done to measure the nature and extent of their suggestive value. To establish this, Dr. Louis Lassagna, of Johns Hopkins, and a team at the Massachusetts Hospital in Boston, gave 162 patients just off the operating table a concealed alteration of morphine shots and placebo shots. Better than half of the patients got relief from their pain from the inert shots, according to a report in *Scientific American*. A few found their pain had completely vanished. Similar investigations confirmed the fact that suggestion has great therapeutic power.

A reference to the phenomenon of hypnosis may help in understanding the role of autosuggestion in controlling subconscious activity. A great deal of controlled research is being done in this field, which has nothing whatever in common with the parlor entertainment or medicine show brand of hypnotism. In hypnosis the thing that happens seems to be this: As the result of suggestion on the part of the operator, and susceptibility (or acceptance) on the part of the subject, the latter's conscious mind steps aside, its function and activity temporarily suspended, and a direct channel to the subconscious is opened. In this state, suggestions and directions can be planted directly in the subconscious area.

Judged by ordinary standards, the human mind is capable of unusual activity when suggestions are given during a hypnotic trance. An individual when hypnotized was told to do a particular thing at the expiration of 123 days. During this period he was occasionally put under hypnotic trance and would then correctly state the number of days already passed and the number of days that still remained before the day appointed for doing the suggested act. As usual in such cases, he knew nothing about the matter in his waking condition. This suggests that there seemed to be a continuing stream of subconscious activity which is capable not only of remembering instructions received in the hypnotic state, but which is also conscious of the passage of time.

Braid, one of the early researchers in this field, had as one of his hypnotic subjects a young working girl who did not know the grammar of her own language and who had never been taught music. Notwithstanding these facts, this untaught girl under hypnosis correctly accompanied Jenny Lind, the great singer, in several songs in different languages.

There is complete evidence that hypnotic trance can produce analgesia—insensitivity to pain. Outstanding surgeons report cases which show that in postsurgical treatment when intensely painful tissue damage is present, hypnosis permits exercise and other forms of therapy without pain or suffering. In one such reported case a woman's arm had been severely burned when a gas heater exploded. After removal of the dead tissue, for the patient to regain the use of her arm, exercise was ordered. Even with the use of the strongest drugs available, the pain was so intense that the muscles could not be contracted. Under hypnosis the patient felt no pain when told to exercise her arm. She was told that when she woke she would continue the exercise but that it would cause no pain. Awakened from the trance the patient continued to move her arm without pain. Full recovery resulted.

Under hypnotic trance the effect of an anesthetic previously administered can be reversed. A hospital patient whose leg had been completely immobilized by the use of drugs was told that he could walk. This he did in a perfectly normal manner.

Anesthesia induced by suggestions during hypnotic trance has a long and successful record. Beginning about 1840, Dr. James Esdaile in India performed thousands of painless operations using hypnosis. Today many dental and surgical operations are done by this method. Many physicians of high professional standing use suggestions made during hypnotic trance to ease or remove labor pains during the delivery of babies.

Two investigators at the Menninger Foundation recently reported, "Almost every syndrome which we might now label 'psychosomatic' has been reported successfully treated by direct suggestion" [1] (under hypnosis).

It has been definitely established that posthypnotic behavior occurs. This is shown in three phases of hypnotic phenomena. There is irrefutable evidence of the ability of a person in trance to recall, upon waking, conditions occurring during hypnosis. There is also the strange ability to carry out suggestions given during the hypnotic trance. There are numerous completely authenticated instances of posthypnotic suggestions being carried out after a lapse of five years or more. Perhaps the most significant is the ability during hypnotic trance for a person to recall events of past experience long since faded from the conscious mind.

Hypnotic phenomena described in previous paragraphs have been established by competent investigators both in Europe and America during recent years. These occurrences make necessarily evident an underlying basic part of the mind with unusual power to control and change both physiological and psychological activity when the conscious mind with its ideas of limitation is repressed

[1] Margaret Brenman & Merton M. Gill, *Hypotherapy, A Survey of the Literature.* (The Menninger Foundation Monograph Series Number 5.)

or set aside temporarily. These facts offer a challenge to psychiatrists, psychologists and those in the field of the behavioral sciences. When fully understood and correctly applied in a professional manner, these data offer new methods in therapy, training and character-forming activity.

A remarkable illustration of the power of the subconscious mind to receive and act upon suggestions is found in a report by a five-man team of psychiatrists and surgeons at the University of Texas Southwestern Medical School, Dallas, and reported in the *Journal of the American Medical Association* of May, 1955.

Hypnotism can be used to speed recovery of severely burned patients. Many of these patients were slowly starving because they had lost all appetite. After hypnotic suggestions that they would be hungry and crave food, they regained their appetites, some patients consuming more than 8,000 calories a day.

Instead of begging for drugs to relieve pain, these patients were able to tolerate the pain of skin graft operations without anesthetics while under hypnosis. As a result of the increased food consumption, skin graft adhered and the burns healed much more rapidly. One patient, bedridden for eighteen months, his condition slowly deteriorating, was discharged from the hospital walking and with nearly all his wounds healed, only twelve weeks after hypnosis was started.

What are the implications of this factual report by competent authorities? It must first be observed that going under a hypnotic trance does not cure or change a person in any way. Hypnotism is not a cure for any condition. Two significant things occurred. First, by use of hypnosis the conscious mind of these patients was completely set aside. The activity of this part of their minds was held completely in abeyance. This meant that the fear, the dread, the sure conviction that they could not be healed and get well was also held in abeyance. Second, under hypnosis, these medical men could speak directly to the subconscious mind of these patients. Because the conscious mind with all its ideas of limitation was completely inactive, the creative subconscious mind could bring all its power to sustain and support the healing process.

It is true that the suggestions given by the physicians did not constitute autosuggestions, as used in this chapter; nevertheless, the suggestions directed to the subconscious minds of these patients activated energies resident in the human body and brought about speedy and almost miraculous recovery.

It must be stated again that the subconscious mind not only hears the words used but it knows exactly whether or not the conscious mind believes what it is saying. The subconscious mind is limited (and this is very important) by the degree of conviction in the conscious mind. Quite apart from hypnosis, if an individual could arrive at an absolute conviction regarding any matter, the subconscious mind would accept and act upon the statement and desire of the conscious mind just as effectively as would be the case in hypnotic trance, regardless of how deep the trance.

The truly scientific mind accepts a fact whether or not it knows how or why it came to be a fact. It is not greatly important that we do not know just how or why an assumption of well-being, of good health, or of success will influence the subconscious mind and start its creative power working to bring about these conditions. That it does so work, and that definite and specific results are achieved, is not open to question; it has been demonstrated in many thousands of lives.

The role of autosuggestion is perhaps the most important method of giving direction to your subconscious, as well as that of creating healthy emotional attitudes. It should be remembered that the subconscious not only hears what you say, but it knows fully what you believe and how you feel. The conscious part of mind may misunderstand the message that emerges from the subconscious, but the reverse is never true. You cannot deceive or mislead your subconscious. Your every thought, positive or negative, constructive or destructive, forms the raw material upon which subconscious energy works. Placing a negative thought in your subconscious is like dropping a poison tablet into a vessel of water from which you must drink.

When an idea is expressed by the spoken word, empowered by expectancy and strong conviction, it makes a greater impression upon the subconscious than when the same thought is simply held loosely in the mind. Repeated spoken expressions of purpose or desire make a cumulative impact upon the subconscious.

This process of studying a problem thoroughly, thereby filling the subconscious mind with facts to be used in solving the problem or furnishing creative material, is similar to the modern process of feeding facts into an electronic computer to be used in arriving at the solution of a given problem.

These modern computers use only the facts fed into them, just as the subconscious mind has available only those thoughts, feelings and facts fed into it by the conscious mind. The computer usually comes up with correct answers. The subconscious always does.

Consider the following experience reported by the *British Medical Journal*:

> Since birth the skin below the neck of a 16-year-old boy had been as hard and crusty as fish scales. Every skill known to medical science had been applied without results. As a last resort, the boy was hypnotized and told that the condition on his left arm would presently disappear.
>
> Five days later the horny area on the arm peeled off and the skin became soft and pink. Subsequent hypnotic suggestions cleared the scales from most of his arm and leg surface. What strange subconscious powers brought about this cure, a cure admittedly beyond the skill of medical science!

When a suggestion is made directly to the subconscious mind without interference from the conscious mind, such a suggestion can completely inhibit and prevent the normal functioning of the conscious part of the mind. This fact may, in part, account for some forms of compulsive action which individuals seem to be utterly unable to prevent. It may also account, at least in part, for certain kinds of behavior found in some forms of mental illness.

The ability of the subconscious mind to completely inhibit the normal functioning of the conscious mind is illustrated by the following widely reported incident: Madame Koo, of the Chinese National Embassy, gave a party just prior to a flight to Bangkok. It was a small party for a few of her more intimate friends. A young Washington hypnotist named George W. Hardy was engaged to furnish entertainment for Madame Koo's guests.

During the course of the evening, Hardy hypnotized a young woman, one of the guests who had volunteered. While the young lady was under hypnotic trance, Hardy told her that she would not be able to see Madame Koo when she waked. After some experiments with the girl, in which he demonstrated the power of hypnotic suggestion, he waked her. She seemed perfectly normal and told some of the guests of her experience in going under trance. She then mixed with other guests, as if nothing had happened.

Later in the evening Madame Koo approached the girl and offered her a glass of orange juice. The girl gave a loud shriek and then covered her face in embarrassment. The other guests rushed to her side. "What is the matter?" they asked. In a very nervous state the girl replied, "A glass came toward me." "Who was holding it?" several guests asked almost at the same time. "Nobody," said the girl, swaying dizzily to her chair.

The posthypnotic suggestion was so effective that the girl failed again and again to see Madame Koo. She was rehypnotized and assured that she would see Madame Koo when she waked. On emerging from trance the second time, the girl was free of her negative hallucination and recognized Madame Koo on her first appearance.

This method of direct suggestion to the subconscious mind is older than medicine. It was used before medicine men had separated from the priesthood. Suggestions as a method of relieving pain and controlling the mind were used more than three thousand years ago in India. The British Museum has a bas-relief taken from a tomb in Thebes showing an Egyptian hypnotist and his patient. There is a tradition that the father of medicine, Aesculapius, used this method to relieve pain.

The glib assumption by many people that autosuggestion is simply a method of fooling one's self is not supported by realistic, scientific study.

The president of the Parapsychology Foundation of New York has made this revealing statement: "Suggestion is not only a method of treatment for psychological abnormalities, however, but is at once the cause as well as the cure of them. It is the source of our highest aspirations and our best achievements; it is the seed of all the bright and dark activities of human beings in this world. We find our way through life by following suggestions that are constantly being made to consciousness, either by ourselves or by the people and events in the outer world. Suggestion is the key to all education and the root of value in all experience." [2]

The force of repeated suggestions made to the subconscious mind should be varied in tone and in verbal expression. There are only eight notes in the musical scale, yet from the variation of these eight notes, millions of compositions have been written, each reflecting the thought and the emotions of the composer. Some melodies are written in the major key and some in the minor. For the composer, his understanding of both life and music influence what his inner ear hears and what is produced in his music.

When we begin to understand the mental and emotional notes of our mind, we shall be able to produce more harmonius life compositions. It should be remembered that anger, fear and condemnation, jealousy and self-pity strike only discords that jangle our whole being out of tune. It is when our charge and direction to the subconscious is based on the full scale of life, that is inherent in each person, that we can organize and direct our life as though it were a glorious symphony producing only harmony.

To understand the influence of autosuggestion, recall the fact that you express yourself through two largely independent systems of nerves. The central nervous system is by and large the instrument used by the conscious mind. You also express yourself through what is known as the autonomic nervous system. This part of the body organism has two aspects. One is known as the sympathetic nervous system. This is the creative, action-producing, accelerating part of the apparatus by which you express yourself. The second part of the autonomic system is known as the parasympathetic system. Its function is to give balance and stability. If its opposite part,

[2] Eileen J. Garrett, *Awareness* (New York: Farrar, Straus & Cudahy, Inc.). Used by permission.

the sympathetic apparatus, becomes too active its function is to apply the brakes, to slow down, and frequently to produce a calm vegetative attitude or condition.

Further it should be recognized that the autonomic nervous system is, to a very large degree, controlled by the subconscious. It follows then that repeated spoken affirmations of a constructive nature will produce a continuing and increasing impression in your subconscious. The fact that emotionally empowered thought has a direct and immediate impact upon bodily functions is too well known to require supporting data.

Affirmations which express the sincere conviction of the conscious mind, and are repeated from time to time, create a reservoir of subconscious power which in turn strengthens and gives stability to the original assumption of the conscious mind.

People frequently make the mistake of assuming that the repetition of a given affirmation, for instance, Coué's famous statement, "Every day in every way, I am getting better and better," is all that is needed. It cannot be too strongly emphasized that, for an affirmation to be effective, the spoken words or statements must embody sane intellectual conviction and strong emotional support or acceptance. For less thoughtful people, a given memorized statement may be the only method they can use, and certainly this has some value. For the man or woman who is determined to achieve outstanding results, the affirmation should be changed and enriched in its expression from time to time. Expressing the same thing in different words means that the conscious mind is actively engaged in the process. Spoken words express not only your desire but also convey your emotional tone when you are attempting to plant an idea or concept upon which your subconscious is to work.

Recall again that the subconscious mind does not reason inductively. It works from the general to the particular. Your affirmation, therefore, should be in the form of a general statement or principle. Do not attempt to tell your subconscious how it is to solve the problem or by what method it is to bring to you the resources you want.

By the very nature of mind this creative function belongs to the subconscious.

The time and manner of projecting an affirmation are important. Physical as well as mental and emotional relaxation is necessary. Hundreds of books by well-know psychologists give effective techniques for relaxing body and mind. Relaxation is necessary to have "peace of mind." Only a calm, assured state of mind can produce constructive results.

The time for expressing affirmations is also important. Remember that the subconscious never sleeps—it is always active. It follows then that just before going to sleep in the evening is the time when the expression of affirmations achieves maximum results. Let go of the frustrations, disappointments and concerns of the day. Then express with conviction, expectancy and confidence the charge which you want to give your subconscious. When this is done continue to relax and sleep.

A quiet period during the early morning before you address yourself to the problems of the day is perhaps the second most effective time for implanting suggestions in your subconscious. Once this is done in a thoughtful, confident manner, turn to the usual problems and responsibilities of the day and forget the matter. During the day while your conscious mind is busy with the job or whatever task you face, subconscious mentation will occur, and the results of this creative thinking may come to you at the most unusual times and in the most unorthodox fashion.

However, it is not assumed that every person can or will apply this method of autosuggestion with equal success; for certainly the process requires faith and perseverance. It is of little value to direct an affirmative idea of well-being to the subconscious and at the same time cross our fingers in recognition of the fact that we do not believe what we are saying. Sincerity, scientific impartiality, along with something like the unspoiled faith of a child, are necessary. And one must not be discouraged if results are not immediately apparent.

Many, if not most, of us have consciously used our subconscious mind so little, in the sense of giving it orders, that it is a rusty instrument. But, just as a rusty machine will respond to lubrication and use, so the subconscious mind will gain steadily in flexibility and dependability when lubricated with intelligent faith and used with persistence.

In the process of building and directing subconscious activity, you must keep at the center of your consciousness the fact that the human mind is the richest unexplored area of the world. Our subconscious minds, like the land on which we live, do not care what we plant. Good or bad, they return to us enhanced, the potential of what we plant. Years ago Holmes in his poem, "The Chambered Nautilus" expressed in meaningful fashion this concept of life enriched by self-direction:

"Build thee more stately mansions, O, my soul,
        As the swift seasons roll!
    Leave thy low-vaulted past!
Let each new temple nobler than the last,
Shut thee from heaven with a dome more vast,
        Till thou at length art free,
Leaving thine outgrown shell by Life's unresting sea."

10
THE MIND IS
FATHER OF THE DISEASE

THE human body functions in response to mental energy. The mind controls every activity occurring within the body organism. Every cell with its myriad processes, every tissue, and every organ —glands, heart and brain—all are activated and controlled by mental and emotional ideas and concepts.

The intensity and duration of the response to mental power projected by the mind are largely determined by the strength of the emotional force by which they are empowered. It should be recognized that every thought or mental image has an emotional or feeling content. You cannot think without feeling and you cannot express an emotion that does not have as its inciting cause a movement of mental energy. Mind action precedes physical processes. The endocrine glands exhibit this drama of physical action caused and controlled by mental and emotional stimuli.

The nature or content of mind determines how and what organs of the body will receive and the kind of response that will be made. Constructive thinking—thoughts that are directed to the accomplishment of a goal or strongly held objective—stimulate and integrate all body processes. Thinking incited by situations of fear, doubt, anxiety and frustration has a debilitating effect upon health and normal well-being.

Every *erg* of mental and emotional energy projected by the mind must produce a result in keeping with its nature and strength. A well-known law of physics applies in the field of mental action just as unfailingly as in physical science. Every action must produce an equal and corresponding reaction. An equally challenging consideration is the fact that energy—mental or physical—is never lost —never goes out of existence. Energy spent is contained and conserved in the action or effort it produces.

One outstanding author, Dr. Franz Alexander, Director of the Chicago Institute of Psychoanalysis, has a meaningful statement:

> The fact that the mind rules the body is, in spite of its neglect by biology and medicine, the most fundamental fact which we know about the process of life. . . . The body, that complicated machine, carries out the most complex and refined motor activities under the influence of such psychological phenomena as ideas and wishes.[1]

It is recognized by outstanding medical authorities that not less than 75 per cent of all cases of ill health are due to mental and emotional causes. It is a matter of common observation that a person's mental and emotional life objectifies itself in the condition of his body and in his environment.

Perhaps the most famous dog in canine history was the one owned by Pavlov, the Russian research scientist. The idea that the physiological processes of the dog's body could be "conditioned" to respond by repeated stimuli form the basis of a concept that is imbedded deeply in medical and educational thinking. Everyone would expect a dog's glands to salivate at the sight and smell of food. However, until Pavlov completed his experiments, it was never assumed that a stimulus not in any way connected with food would produce this automatic salivation. This Russian scientist devised an ingenious experiment, simple but effective. He would place meat before his dogs and just before allowing them to have the meat, he would ring a bell. In a very short time, whenever the bell rang,

---

[1] Dr. Franz Alexander, *Psychosomatic Medicine, Its Principles and Applications* (Chicago, Ill.: American Publishers, Corp.).

the dogs' glands would secrete saliva. Meat or no meat, the bell alone stimulated those glands in the dogs' mouths. Their glands responded to a mere bell, a signal not found in nature, exactly as they reacted to the sight and smell of food.

Pavlov discovered that glandular responses, an automatic function of the body, not under the conscious mind, could be trained to respond to artificial stimulus. This process is now known throughout medical literature as a "conditioned reflex."

Other scientists in Europe and America have continued the same line of experimentation on human subjects with the result that it is now known that human beings can be conditioned to respond to an artificial stimulus when this stimulus is repeated a sufficient number of times.

By the very nature of these experiments it is evident that this conditioned reflex is the result of a mental and emotional response rather than a reaction to chemical or physical stimuli.

The conditioned reflex is then another example of the relationship between conscious and subconscious mind and emotional activity. The conscious mind believes and feels that a given experience, or idea, has meaning and value. This concept is planted in the subconscious mind by repetition. This in turn makes the response automatic, that is, a suggestion planted in the subconscious mind becomes a part of the energy and directing force which controls all the natural forces of the human body.

The conditioned reflex may be used to build up positive reactions regarding any situation. On the other hand, it may become a disorganizing negative force in the life of the individual. Centering the attention of the conscious mind on the processes of the body tends to disrupt the competent functioning of the autonomic nervous system. The complex processes of the human body are not and cannot be directed by the conscious mind. This part of the mind can only influence these processes through subconscious activity. It is a matter of common observation that if one holds his finger on the pulse, the heart will change its beat and a normally functioning stomach will "act up" if it is the object of scrutiny by the conscious mind.

Mental concepts, or ideas, are not the lifeless things they appear to be to many people. Mental and emotional activity are not merely blocks of intellectual property that can be locked up or ignored at will. Mental activity continues as a part of the personality and cannot be discarded according to the caprice of the moment. Mental and emotional activity are a part of our personality and these forces do things. If improperly directed, they are capable of astonishing results—results which have no apparent relation to the ideas or mental concepts responsible for them. The proper control of mental and emotional activity is a matter of health as well as a moral duty.

Since the autonomic nervous system, as well as the glandular process of the body, is under the control of the subconscious mind, if the subconscious mind is given wrong or improper directions by the conscious mind, the organs of the body will "act up" and the nervous system will carry the wrong messages. It is important to realize that the nerves are simply telegraph wires. They are only responsible for the messages that are given to them to carry. Behind the wires is the man behind the body, the operator, and upon him rests the responsibility for the way the nervous system and all physiological processes of the body function. The trouble is not with the mechanism of the body but with "the mind in back of the mind." When the mental and emotional processes of the individual are improperly directed, the man behind the body is in trouble and he has no way of showing this trouble except through the various organs of his body. The cause of nervous disorders, of whatever make or kind, is in the personality in the realm of ideas and not in the human body.

The basic consideration in this matter is the fact that conditioned reflexes are caused by mental and emotional processes. The basis of this conditioning is subconscious activity.

The fact that a mental movement of the conscious mind directed to the subconscious will bring about organic changes in tissues of the body is dramatically illustrated by experiments with people under hypnosis. This type of experiment has been carried out by many different researchers, all with the same result.

Recall that a common parlor trick of hypnosis is to suggest to a subject in trance that he is about to be burned with a red hot needle. If, following this suggestion, a cold needle is placed against his skin, he will cry out in pain and what is more remarkable, the skin will exhibit the characteristic blister as if it had been actually burned. On the other hand, if a patient in a hypnotic trance is actually touched with a red hot needle but suggestion is made that the needle is, in fact, cold, he may appear to feel nothing and have no characteristic blister afterwards.

We ordinarily assume that this power of the mind over body operates through suggestion. A better term would be that it operates by direct action incited by the subconscious mind. It is frequently the case that when some people are told that their symptoms will disappear, their symptoms do disappear. Others are capable by the action of their mind to produce their own symptoms. A well-authenticated source reports that a convict could reproduce on his body the signs of the Zodiac at will. There are, of course, numerous stories of mystics who have reproduced the stigmata. These facts actually occur, indicating the power of mind over the physiologic processes of the human body.

H. J. Eysneck has reported an experiment on two groups of children with warts, one of which was given orthodox medical treatment and the other treated by suggestion. The procedure was to draw a picture of the child's hand with the wart on it on a large sheet of paper, and then with a certain amount of suggestions, drawing a circle around the wart and reducing its size day by day until the wart had completely disappeared from the picture. The result of the experiment was that treatment by suggestion proved far more effective than the orthodox medical therapy.

Malignant tumors constitute a threat to health and life for a significant segment of our population. There are some authorities who believe that cancer is the result of a misdirected emotional drive. This emotional drive, it is believed, turns the individual's life force into self-destructive energy. Since a force of this kind is subconscious, it often appears in direct opposition to what the conscious mind of the patient desires. This process may be due to some heavy sense of guilt long repressed and exhibits itself in a person who has climbed to the top of his chosen occupation but has gained no real satisfaction as the result of his success. It is quite possible that ambition may turn on a man and destroy him through the mechanism of concern, the individual himself sustaining and nourishing his own destructive guest.

There is a great body of data supporting the idea that the course of cancer can be altered by the patient's mental and emotional reactions to his illness. In medical thinking, once the malignant processes get beyond a certain stage, there are no physical means of stopping it. There are well-proven instances in which apparently inoperable or incurable cancers have stopped spreading. In many cases no reason is apparent. In other cases, the individual believed that through willpower or faith the cancer was brought under control. It is a matter of common experience among medical men that imponderables do at times alter the course of illness after all known physical treatments have failed.

Certainly we live in an age of stress. The code through which our culture is expressed results in many powerful emotions, fear, aggression, guilt or other forms of antisocial behavior which cannot find expression or relief. Since Freud, we have known that the human mind can repress such impulses but after being repressed they may express themselves in various other ways, in neurosis or in mental or physical illness. Stress of this kind not only adds to the normal stress of living but the individual, being unaware of processes which are subconsciously projected, cannot regulate them.

Where a stress situation is created for the individual by an emotional disturbance, the reasons for which he does not understand, it is difficult, if not impossible, to avoid its impact.

The symptoms of subconscious disturbances frequently take a negative form—anxiety, frustration, guilt, tension, or depression. On the other hand, they may be expressed in a more positive way, the psychosis and neurosis, which is ordinarily thought of as actual illness. It is known that at times an illness may require physical symptoms. This is accomplished by activating certain bodily processes for which no physical cause can be found.

A subconscious disturbance may in some instances not be the actual cause of illness. The cause may be found in germs, irritants, or in some traumatic accident. Under normal conditions the wisdom of the body would give appropriate warning through the nervous system to the mind and the proper forces would be dispatched to deal with them. The production of antibodies is the result of this process, but if the mind is disturbed and confused by a subconscious conflict, it may not be able to muster sufficient forces, or it may give wrong or confused orders.

If the mental and emotional disturbance is sufficiently severe, the illness may be welcomed in an attitude of what amounts to subconscious suicide.

The most prevalent affliction experienced by the American people is fatique—frequently termed "depression" by medical men. The extent of this ubiquitous mental and emotional disease is indicated by the millions of prescriptions issued for tranquilizing drugs and the additional millions of nonprescription items sold, not only in pharmacies but in grocery stores and gasoline stations. Perhaps as many as 100,000,000 individuals seek to find in alcohol an elixir for all troubles of mind and body, including fatigue or "depression."

Many people suffer all the time from fatigue. They are always tired. Energy runs low early in the morning, the remainder of the day is simply "dragged out." Tiredness is the great affliction of the mediocre, the average, the unsuccessful. Strangely enough, these are the people who are always bored. The thrill of the job has long since been lost. To them the business of life is unrelieved drudgery.

What's wrong with these people? Have they less ability or less training? Are they sick? Psychiatry, a science devoted to the study of mental and emotional processes as observed in the business of living, has very unorthodox views about this fatigue or tiredness idea. These hardheaded scientists have very little sympathy for tired people. They believe that because of a lack of interest and desire and the resulting boredom, people ordinarily use only the top layers of their supply of energy.

Professor Edward Thorndike of Columbia University stated, "Boredom is the only real cause of diminution of work." The

Fatigue Laboratory at Harvard University has announced the conclusion that "The phenomenon formerly called fatigue is better described as boredom. It is boredom that causes a reduced rate of working." Now why are people bored? Negative thinking, indolence or lack of ambition, ignorance of essential facts about the job are some of the answers for some of the victims of boredom. The plain fact is that some people don't want to work. They would rather enjoy the small comforts of failure than to purchase success at the price of sustained work. Some people love the despondency of failure and limitation more than they love the achievements of creative, hard work.

In general terms there are five evident facts about this state of body and mind:

1. Fatigue is not the result of too much work or too hard work.

2. Fatigue does not mean that a person's supply of energy is exhausted.

3. Rest will not cure fatigue.

4. Less work will not prevent fatigue.

5. Leisure and money will not prevent or cure fatigue.

Some people fear a nervous breakdown if they work hard. Consider what Dr. A. A. Brill, one of our great psychiatrists—and, incidentally, a man who worked on the average of sixteen hours every day—had to say: "No one ever suffers a nervous breakdown from overwork. These maladies simply do not exist." Yet it is true that work can cause fatigue or even a nervous breakdown. These are not caused, however, by the amount or the intensity of the work. They are the end-results of uninspired efforts, of boredom and resentment. In a nutshell, work is not the cause and rest is not the cure.

As the phophet Isaiah well knew, nature is not stingy. She has given the human race no meager inheritance. The normal human body has stored within itself enough energy to meet any demands that are likely to be made upon it, coming either from the monotony of the daily grind or from the excitement of any sudden emergency. The truth is, nature never runs on a narrow margin. She does not do business on a limited capital. She does not start the human engine with insufficient steam to complete the journey. Not lack of capacity, but boredom and frustration are the cause of that tired feeling, that condition of fatigue and listlessness which afflicts so many people.

One of the things we need to remember is that when we experience fatigue, even when we are "dog tired," we still have a lot of unused energy. Another fact is that true or normal fatigue is a chemical affair, it is the result of recent effort, physical, mental or emotional. It is the result of feelings caused by the presence of waste materials in the muscles and in the blood. The whole picture becomes clear if we think of the human organism as a factory whose fires continuously burn, yielding heat and energy together with certain waste materials, carbon dioxide and ash. These waste products that follow physical and mental effort are removed in one night of sound sleep.

The human body as well as the mental and emotional apparatus have a built-in mechanism for renewal and replacing of the supply of energy. However, if the conscious mind fills the subconscious with thoughts and emotions expressing boredom, fatigue and frustration, this part of the mind, being creative and under the direct control of the self-aware part of mind, will direct its energy to create conditions and feelings reflecting the orders it receives from the volitional and directive area of mind. We create fatigue and boredom and frustration by our thinking. To change the condition, change the conscious mind picture which produces the sense of failure and depletion of energy.

The human body has a built-in thermostat which maintains the inner physical temperature at 98.6 degrees; this, regardless of the temperature in the environment. The surrounding weather may be either freezing cold or 110 degrees, yet this built-in thermostat enables your body to maintain its own climate. The function of this built-in mechanism is to enable the body not to reflect the climate of its environment. Cold or hot, this thermostat maintains its own level in the absence of opposing physical conditions or mental activity.

It is equally evident that a person has a built-in mental and emotional thermostat which makes it possible to maintain an emotional climate and atmosphere in spite of disturbing situations in which you find yourself. Many people, of course, do not use this mental and emotional thermostat—some do not know that such a thing is possible and they do not understand that they have a built-in power of self-direction.

When a person lives with the constant anticipation of ill health and continually imagines pictures of failure and frustration, this mental thermostat functions at the level of our thoughts and feelings, thus we experience bodily ills, fatigue and depression and other debilitating conditions.

The activity of mind is two-fold: The conscious mind selects and determines what it wants and this action of the conscious mind is then placed in the deep layers of the subconscious mind which proceeds to create conditions and circumstances in keeping with the charge given it by the conscious part of the mind. Self-confidence, courage and expectancy are the result of a positive attitude entertained by the conscious mind and thus placed within the creative aspect of subconscious mind.

It is true that we cannot see the subconscious mind. There is no automatic mechanism by which we can determine its content. However, we can recognize that the creative energy of the subconscious responds to the demands made upon it by the conscious mind. Since the conscious mind is the self-aware, self-starting aspect of our personality, we do, in fact, have within our control a built-in apparatus by which we can influence not only circumstances in our environment but, directly and indirectly, the internal processes of the human body.

11

SUBCONSCIOUS MENTATION AND YOUR EMOTIONS

YOU remember that Alice in Wonderland talked with a grinning Cheshire cat with a head and no body. When we talk of mental health, we, of course, are thinking of the health of the mind, but no one ever saw a mind which was not associated with a person, equipped with organs, bones, muscles, nerve cells and all the numerous structures which make up the human being. No mind ever went by itself to the office or shop. Minds that are so sick that they must go to a mental hospital take their bodies along with them.

As a person you are not two things—mind and body. The mind has a direct influence on body processes. You are not a body and a mind. You are b-o-d-y-m-i-n-d. The two work together and influence each other. Health and illness are conditions experienced by you.

The mind expresses itself in two ways—it thinks and it feels. Mental activity is a blend of thought and emotion. The mind never thinks without feeling and it never feels without thinking.

Mental and emotional activity can change the chemistry, function and structure of the human body. The emotion of anger is a good example of this fact. When a person is angry, visible and external bodily changes occur—the face gets red, the eyelids get wide, the lips tighten, the fists clench and the hands tremble.

But striking as these outside changes may be, the changes within the body are even greater and often have an obvious purpose. For instance, when a person becomes angry, the blood clots more quickly than under normal conditions. The purpose is evident— an angry person may fight; in a fight a wound is likely; a wound means bleeding, and in bleeding rapid clotting is a decided advantage.

In anger the red blood count jumps up as much as a half million; the spleen contracts; the muscles of the stomach squeeze down hard and one of the endocrine glands releases into the blood stream large amounts of adrenalin. The heart increases its rate to as high as 100 to 200 beats per minute. The blood pressure leaps upward, so much that at times a person dies of a ruptured cerebral vessel during a fit of anger.

In the same way other mental and emotional activities, such as anxiety, fear, worry, hate, disgust and frustration bring about changes in the normal processes of the body and may produce the experience of illness.

Everyone fully accepts the idea that physical disease may be caused by the wrong kind of food. But the idea that physical disease can be produced by the wrong kind of emotions is not commonly understood and is rejected by many people. More important, few of us know that fully half of all aliments we have are emotionally induced. This estimate is conservative.

The first thing is to recognize and act on this fact: Your mind is its own boss. You think what you want to think. You feel what you want to feel. No one and no thing can invade and condition your mind unless you are willing. You select and produce your mental and emotional activity.

By using common sense you can avail yourself of many medical aids to keep your body in good physical condition. Some of these things you can do for yourself. In most cases you need the assistance of your physician. In the same way, you can do much to keep your mental and emotional activity sound and healthy. Why not study and safeguard the processes of your mind in the same way you do your body? You would not knowingly eat poisoned food or come into close contact with tuberculosis germs. The wrong kind of mental and emotional activity can produce conditions which are equally dangerous to your life and working ability. Why not select your mental and emotional food with at least the same care and good sense that you use when you go to the grocery store!

Scientific delving into personalities has brought forth the fact that arthritis, which is just about as physical a condition as one could have, is in many cases directly traceable to thwarted ambition or disturbed emotions. In fact the close connection between emotions and illness has become well-established.

For instance, a man, son of a successful father, had taken his own capital to another city and started in business. He was not a good businessman; he failed. He shrank from the idea of returning to his father and being subjected to the latter's scorn. Soon he developed arthritis. No treatment helped until a farseeing doctor found the emotional cause. Recent medical annals are filled with recoveries from such conditions when the patient is taught to understand how they have their origin.

In another case a very successful man in his middle thirties enjoyed good health but was greatly disturbed whenever he was assigned to take a business trip to a particular city some distance away. This emotional disturbance showed itself in a variety of physical symptoms of distressing nature, and finally developed into a heart condition. His physician discovered that the symptoms usually subsided after the trip had been made. This was the key to the problem.

It seems that several years previously the young man had been sent on an important business trip to this city, had dismally failed in his mission, and had become extremely distressed at his failure. Now, whenever he received orders to go out again, the memory of his previous failure and its accompanying pain were revived. Buried in the deeper levels of his subconscious mind during his active business days, it had gradually faded in memory, as unpleasant experiences tend to do. But with the revival of the memory came the revival of the pain. The repressed emotion had to find outlet somewhere, so it selected some organ of his body through which to express.

Life—particularly the emotional side of life—must be expressed. Civilized man, inhibiting his emotions, builds up a "head of steam" that has to blow through safety valves. The internal pressure finds some organ through which it can "blow off." The result is an illness which is physical in expression but emotional in origin.

Emotions rooted in experience of failure, hatred or frustration can and do destroy health. Constructive emotions help to sustain health.

Our emotions are barometers of our mental health. These feeling processes provide symptoms and clues which we can use in judging the health of the illness of the mind. Plato once compared the struggles of the mind to a pair of steeds, each horse attempting to go in a different direction. In the light of modern psychiatric insight we can no longer say that if one makes use of his intelligence and willpower he can control the processes of his mind and his activities. It is a common observation that many highly intellectual and educated individuals fall victims of many powerful emotional demands and desires which submerge their volitional force. It is obvious that a dynamic desire for expression exists which can dominate and assume sovereignty over our actions and thoughts. These uncontrolled drives emerge from the subconscious area of our minds.

It must be recognized that once we have entertained a thought or expressed an emotion, it can never be completely cast out of our personality. If these thoughts and feelings are unacceptable to the conscious mind, they are repressed into the subconscious area of mind. It is equally true that if thoughts and emotions are acceptable to and approved by the conscious mind, they are also deposited in the subconscious mind. However, it is thoughts which are repressed that create problems in human life. Since these repressed thoughts are still alive, their force is used to distort and cripple our conscious controls.

Consider, for example, the information we possess concerning neuroses. Generally defined, a neurosis is a condition in which our conscious mind, its attitudes and activities, are determined by subconscious energy beyond the control of the conscious will. Most neurotic behavior is compulsive behavior and compulsions are usually the product of an unstable or sick mind. Clinical data indicate that our basic motivations may be completely hidden from our conscious awareness. Ordinarily there are times when we do certain things for reasons totally unknown to us.

Those individuals who recognize that the content of the subconscious is determined by their own conscious assumptions usually go through life suppressing and controlling unaccepable thoughts without much difficulty. With some of us, however, a mental and emotional struggle is constantly raging within our subconscious, often resulting in fatigue and exhaustion, for which we can find no reason. Fear, anxiety, depression, excessive guilt, hostility, and powerful uncontrolled needs for love and affection are the result of deep emotional struggle in the subconscious.

Neurotic or psychotic behavior indicates that certain subconscious needs have emerged and overcome the normal controls exercised by the conscious mind. Neurotic behavior is usually a defense against unacceptable subconscious drives which our conscious mind processes have allowed to develop. Sometimes this is our way of dealing with a portion of our real self which we want to hide.

It is frequently true that emotional drives experienced in childhood, due to being suppressed, emerge through the layers of the subconscious and demand expression. There is no guarantee that emotions associated with our childhood will always remain repressed. Our emotional maturity is often limited by anxiety-producing conflicts which we had in early childhood. These conflicts, although hidden in our subconscious, can still influence our behavior and our health.

Childhood patterns can be seen in adults who are prejudiced, egotistical, emotionally frustrated, unduly competitive, inflexible, hostile and guilt-ridden. The need for security, attention and love may be arrested at the childhood level and quite often these repressed needs express themselves in neurotic behavior. In some strange way thoughts repressed during childhood bypass other similar materials and come right through to the conscious level to cause trouble. No one can feel free from the possibility of the emergence of these repressed mental and emotional experiences of childhood at any time. In fact, emotional illness is as unpredictable as a heart attack.

The emotions which we entertain and express may have an obvious and unquestionable impact upon our health or illness, and upon our success or failure, in achieving a satisfactory life experience. It is equally definite that we select not only the thoughts we express but the emotions which we entertain. This selection is done by the conscious mind in its effort to achieve satisfaction at any particular time or any set of circumstances.

The action of the conscious mind is voluntary. Its action and its reaction are determined by itself alone. The conscious mind, by the thoughts which it expresses and the emotions which it entertains, determines how the creative energy of the subconscious will be applied. It must be remembered that the creative energy of the subconscious is impersonal, that it is neutral, and that what it receives from the conscious mind determines the manner in which this energy will be used. The structure and content of personality is determined by this two-fold activity of mind. Inescapably, then, every individual is responsible for that which he experiences. Each individual is, by the very nature of personality structure, the architect of his own destiny. The British statesman, Disraeli, was eminently wise and factual when he said, "Man is not the creature of circumstances. Circumstances are the creature of men."

12
WHY PEOPLE
BEHAVE AS THEY DO

IT was not so long ago that a common drinking glass available near most public water fountains was taken for granted. When the germ theory of disease was first given to the public, people at first rejected the idea. Many would hold the glass up to the light and study it. Since no dangers could be seen, certainly, then, there was nothing dangerous about the glass or the water it contained.

As the idea of sanitation became general, people came to accept the fact that whether they could see danger in it or not, the common drinking glass was a health menace, although the germs could not be seen with the naked eye.

As psychiatry and psychology continue to develop and the average person comes to know something about the structure and functioning of the mind, the same conviction will eventually prevail about motivation and normal mental health. As in the case of the public drinking glass, we cannot see behavior mechanism at work but they are part of human experience and their existence will be fully acknowledged and accepted as we learn more about why we behave as we do.

In the future those who are concerned with directing the work of other people and those individuals who are attempting to live a self-directed life, will recognize that mental and emotional facts are valid, in some ways even more valid than physical facts. It will also be recognized that there are causes for all types of behavior and that these causes more often than not arise in the subconscious area of mind. It follows from this that all behavior, all forms of action, have meaning and purpose. The purpose and meaning of behavior may be partially or completely hidden. The emotional actions and attitudes of the average person are known to be of basic importance in all our varied activities and relationships.

Just as the human body has many physical mechanisms built into it to enable it to survive in its environment, so human personality has developed mental and emotional mechanisms by which it adjusts to change and stress in the experience of life. All individuals are constantly bombarded by mental and emotional stresses or threats arising from their relationships with others. These periods of change and stress tend to upset our balance and produce anxiety, fear and frustration. The ability to understand and to maintain mental and emotional relationships are vitally necessary if a person is to experience a satisfactory self-directed life.

It should be noted on the other hand that the influence of our relationships to others is by no means limited to traumatic impact. In these relationships we find support, encouragement, and enhancement of all our efforts.

The Danish philosopher, Sören Kierkegaard, once said, "Life is an examination, a test." It is in this testing experience that many of our conflicts and frustrations, as well as the forces which enhance and stabilize personality are found. In meeting the stresses of life, in order to preserve and restore our mental and emotional balance, we develop and use individual adaptive mechanisms and resort to patterns of behavior which psychologists describe as defense and escape mechanisms.

In evaluating the reason we act as we do, it should be noted that even a person's physical organism, although reasonably stable, is always changing. One's mental and emotional structure is less stable but more dynamic.

Just as the soundness of a house is tested, not by the pleasant skies of summer, but in the storms of winter, the soundness of personality structure is tested by the way we respond to situations in which our needs are blocked and in which we are prevented from achieving our goal. The intensity of the frustration we experience varies with the strength of the need and the duration of its blocking. For instance, the more eager an employee is to be promoted, the more frustrated he becomes if he does not secure the promotion.

An adjustment mechanism is any method habitually used for overcoming difficulties, reaching goals, satisfying needs, or relieving frustrations. These adjustment mechanisms are largely, if not completely, subconscious. It is rare that such a mechanism brings satisfactory results and usually does not bring complete relief from frustration.

Various terms are used in describing these adjustment mechanisms. Five terms ordinarily used are: "repression," "aggression," "rationalization," "compensation" and "projection." These are usually described as adjustment mechanisms. The term "negativism," "fantasy" and "regression" are frequently described as escape mechanisms.

Perhaps the term "repression" describes the mechanism most often used. This process of forgetting includes mental and emotional activities, which are not acceptable to the conscious mind. If removed from conscious awareness by processes of which the individual is not directly aware, the repression is frequently a defense mechanism against anxiety or guilt. Experiences that are so unacceptable to the conscious mind that they cannot be tolerated in awareness are automatically and without conscious action stored in the subconscious mind. However, if an experience is unacceptable to the conscious mind and is *purposefully* placed in the subconscious mind and forgotten, this is called "suppression." It is a voluntary or self-aware activity.

The term "aggression" usually describes the action of a person who is consciously or subconsciously trying to hurt or destroy what he believes to be the source of his frustration. This aggressive process may be directed to other persons or to other things. The more harmful element in this process occurs when the individual directs his aggressive impulse upon himself.

In the mechanism known as "projection," a person subconsciously attributes one's own traits, attitudes and activity to other persons. Other persons are seen through the lens of the mind of the individual who is using the projective mechanism.

In the mechanism known as "displacement," the process is simply one of attaching an effect to something other than its proper object or cause. For instance, the hatred of a child for his father may be attached to a walking stick used by the father. Frequently anger aroused by punishment is transferred to a pet, or to other persons.

In "rationalization" the individual attempts to form convincing reasons that account for his practices or beliefs when these beliefs or practices are questioned by the person himself or by others. The process of rationalization is not connected with the true motivations which cause the process.

When a person uses the mechanism of "compensation," he is attempting a program of action, the purpose of which is to balance off some lack or loss in some characteristic or status. The process of compensation does not indicate the motivation which brought it about. Freud described compensation as an effort to exclude painful awareness of any deficiency of behavior or personality from the conscious volitional area of mind. Adler's concept is that compensation is an effort to overcome an inferiority complex.

The term "conversion" describes a process which makes up the whole range of psychosomatic disorders. In this process, a physical symptom—hysterical blindness or paralysis, for example—is used as the expression of a mental or emotional conflict.

It is also true that this mechanism of conversion is used to limit the ability of a person to perform efficiently in a particular work situation. In instances of this kind, the process involves a basic emotional conflict in the personality structure. These conflicts are usually grounded in childhood experiences.

In evaluating a limiting behavior pattern, it is necessary to find the cause. Once the cause is found and this, of course, is unknown to the person exhibiting the behavior pattern, the reason for the particular conduct or action is understood and is no longer necessary as an effort to adjust to the realities of life. The reason for this is that the emotional maladjustment which gave rise to the particular emotional pattern had its origin in childhood. When the inciting cause is brought into the conscious mind and understood, the person realizes at once that he is reacting in a child-like manner and that such infantile behavior is no longer desired or needed.

A friend of mine once complained that he could not hold a job, that he was constantly frustrated in his work. Because of this he had developed ideas of inferiority, shame and self-accusation. With professional help an analysis of his childhood personality makeup soon revealed that he was held by a strong mother-fixation.

What this man's subconscious mind, through the mechanism of conversion, was attempting to do was to persuade him that he would be happier at home with his mother, who, he was convinced, was the only person who really loved him and had his interest at heart. His frustration and dissatisfaction in the various jobs he had held during a period of several years was not due to inefficiency; it was the emotional pull to return to his mother that made him inefficient. Through the professional help which he secured, he came to understand that he was really trying to be a child again, and with this insight his ability to achieve satisfaction and success in his job promptly changed. His understanding of the other adult elements in his personality structure, even the emotional ones, made it clear to him that as an individual he was free from the limiting influence of "apron strings."

These limiting behavior patterns can be changed. It is also true that in many, many instances the very handicaps imposed by the behavior mechanism are actually transformed into assets. The person then becomes superior in the very way in which he was formerly inferior and inefficient.

The escape mechanisms usually involve three methods of dealing with problems: "negativism," "fantasy" and "regression." The foundation of the process known as negativism is usually laid in the early relations and experiences with the person's parent. The discipline imposed upon a child by his parents may be so severe that the frustration which the child experiences is in later life expressed in his relations with other adults. He may resist suggestions, insist on small, unimportant points in routine matters, or frequently fail to understand what he is told to do. These are reactions which will appear particularly in his relations with people in authority.

In "fantasy" we use our minds to reduce our frustrations. These efforts may in some instances constitute a realistic process for solving problems. On the other hand, this process also provides an escape from frustration by giving the person an imaginary satisfaction. As an example, hungry men dream of food; others dream of the death of a relative who would leave them money. In such wish-fulfilling thoughts or fantasies, it is sometimes difficult to draw a line between daydreaming and constructive planning. In the same way it is even more difficult to differentiate dreaming from creative thinking. A world without fantasy would be one without literature, drama, music or creative concepts.

The daydreams of neurotic persons are different from those of the normal person. The neurotic daydreamer is usually concerned with results rather than processes that require labor. The more frustrating and difficult the experience of any person happens to be, the more fantasy is used to relieve the frustration.

The third type of escape mechanism is known as "regression." This is simply a method of meeting a difficult situation by behavior which would have been appropriate for a child, but is not for an adult.

As previously indicated, the structure of personality has two basic divisions: (1) the conscious mind, the area of mental activity which relates to experience in the environment of which the person is aware and over which he has control. This part of the structure of personality exercises the power of choice. Through it a person decides what he will or will not do and in general determines by this volitional decision the contents of his experience. (2) the subconscious mind, involving by far the largest part of our mental and emotional activity. It operates without our knowledge and we have no immediate control over this process; the process of control or redirection is indirect. The subconscious mind is the storehouse of forgotten memories, ideas, desires and frustrations, all the mental and emotional activity that has been experienced since birth.

It is ordinarily assumed that our motivations for behaving as we do are consciously determined. Such conscious motivations, however, are the rare exception and not rule. Unless an individual understands the structure of personality as it functions on two levels, the idea of the subconscious may be a blow to a person's sense of independence and superiority because it may seriously threaten his assumption that he is in full control of himself.

The Minister of the Marble Collegiate Church in New York City, Dr. Norman Vincent Peale, tells an interesting story illustrating how things said, or actions observed, during early childhood remain with the person and influence his conduct as an adult.

Spending the summer with his grandfather, he watched how his grandfather closed up the house at night. This elderly person would go around the house carrying a lamp. He would set the lamp down at each door, then carefully lock the door, try the doorknob, step away, go back and try the doorknob again and then go through this ritual a third time. Since his grandfather failed to give him a satisfactory reason for this ritual of closing the doors at night, it made a definite impression upon the mind of the young child.

Dr. Peale tells how the influence of this ritual appeared in his own life. Finding himself alone in his apartment, he prepared to retire, went to the door, locked it, then turned around to return to his bedroom but retraced his steps to the door and tried it again. Moving the second time toward his bedroom door, he found himself returning to the door he had just locked. He immediately realized that a memory was reaching out from the past and influencing his action. He realized that this was the childhood influence of his grandfather looming up out of his deep subconscious and compelling him to do something he did not desire to do. In every industrial situation there is usually a group of employes who are described as "accident-prone" persons. There is convincing evidence that accidents in many instances have for their purpose self-punishment. This conclusion is supported by a report given at a Building Research Institute recently held in Washington, D.C. and presented by a staff member of the Pennsylvania Department of Health. This report indicates that a person who is prone to accidents is usually emotionally unstable and rebellious against authority. Such persons subconsciously desire to punish themselves. Their rebellion against authority is the result of childhood experiences long since repressed in the subconscious. Self-punishment through accidents is apparently an expression of guilt feelings resulting from attitudes of hostility and resentment.

Because of the fact that the subconscious mind records perfectly every emotion and thought expressed by an individual, persons frequently find themselves unable to control, much less understand, the reason for their actions.

To understand other people we must first of all understand ourselves, for each person not only influences others but is also influenced by others. It is by this method of person-to-person communication that our basic needs are expressed. We need to be understood, to be wanted, to be appreciated, to feel a sense of pride and accomplishment, to feel secure, and to feel that we can grow and improve and that we have the freedom and opportunity to do so. On the other hand, we use the art of communication as a defense and protection from danger, whether the danger is real or imagined. The relationship established by communication is also used to safeguard our needs, to protect our feelings, in many instances to conceal our feelings, to maintain distances between individuals as well as to seek fellowship and cooperation.

People bring to every situation all their joys, sorrows, fears, hopes, the quality of their home life and, most important of all, they bring a vast submerged reservoir of motivations, personality mechanisms, deep subconscious drives, and all the deeply embedded experiences of the past years. When a business or industrial executive employs a person, he never hires just a pair of hands or that part of the brain that works solely on electronic equations or market changes. In his relation with the person employed, the executive must deal with the "whole man."

We generally assume that we communicate only in words. Verbal expressions are frequently superficial. A person's behavior can be as true a means of communication as can words, many times even more meaningful and significant. This is true since behavior frequently can express feelings that are not and cannot be presented in words. In all the varied relationships in business and industry, feelings can be communicated on the job by certain types of conduct—for example, aggressiveness, extreme competitiveness, or its opposite, unsatisfactory work, failing to meet schedules and appointments, disorganized work, exaggerated use of humor and irony, unfriendly criticism, repeated accidents, chronic alcoholism, illness and anger.

In instances of deep-seated insecurity or fear there is less chance that speech itself will be a reliable means of communication. A young man received a promotion but as soon as he took the new job, he started to express dissatisfaction. He did not like his new office, most of the time he was cool, aloof and disdainful of his fellow employees. On the surface he seemed unafraid and self-possessed.

Since assuming his new duties, he frequently arrived late for conferences and appeared uneasy and disorganized in presenting his plans. His behavior actually was an expression of fear about his ability to hold the new job and the resulting inner conflict about himself. He was not able to express this fear directly because the emotionally induced fear was such a threat to his job and his future—he could not bear to admit it himself.

In essence, life experience consists of a series of power relationships. The infant starts out by being dependent upon others much more powerful than he. As a result, he learns ways of dealing with authority and power figures, even before he learns to walk.

Our complex individual relationships to authority and to those with power to influence our well-being almost always are subconscious and have their beginning in infancy and childhood. Our reactions and feelings toward those in authority may be changed, molded and adapted; but these childhood experiences and patterns of behavior are a permanent part of our subconscious endowment. The basic attitudes that we develop in infancy toward parents, teachers and others in authority are subconsciously transferred during adult life to other people who have the authority or power to direct our lives. In attempting to understand why we act as we do, our efforts to achieve satisfaction and progress, the difficult but challenging datum of the Delphian oracle, "Know Thyself," is still necessary and valid.

13

MEASURE YOUR
MENTAL HEALTH

THE pathologies found in our culture and social order are disturbingly evident. The crescendo of crime, delinquency, divorce and broken homes, chronic alcoholism, drug addiction and other forms of unsocial behavior are a significant part of the mental and emotional nutrients channeled to the public each day by our mass media of communication.

We are told that no one is responsible for these social pathologies. A man commits murder. Pity the unfortunate chap; he is the victim of a compulsive drive resident in his "unconscious." A youth from a home of culture and abundance steals a car. We are told to be tolerant and understanding. His delinquency is due to some traumatic episode in his very early years. An educated man with status and influence in his community becomes a chronic alcoholic. He is sick. Some deprivation, some unfortunate stress situation created a feeling of insecurity during his early life. He drinks to escape his misery. A man is a trusted employee of a bank for twenty years. Being a man of not inconsiderable skill, he empties the vault of hundreds of thousands of depositors' dollars during the period. What is the cause of his defalcation? Undoubtedly it is due to an instinctual drive planted deep in his "uncon-

scious" mind and over which he has no control. Solution: Put
him on probation and give him heavy doses of psychotherapy.

This concept of the unconscious mind (to use the more sinister
but less correct term) as a deep strata of energy, filled with instinctive currents of malignancy and unsocial patterns of conduct,
has infiltrated our current thinking to the degree that the idea of
the individual being responsible for his actions has become quite
obscure, if not lost. Perhaps the most unfortunate illustrative analogy ever used was Freud's "iceberg" concept of the unconscious
(subconscious) part of the mind—cold, threatening, and fatalistic.
Certainly the 10 per cent of the iceberg above the level of the water
can do nothing to change the direction or destination of the mass
of floating ice. Obviously Freud did not intend this impression to
be created. However, when the awesome term "unconscious" is
used, for many people it indicates energy in action over which no
control can be exercised.

Notwithstanding the long overdue necessity for educational
publicity and information regarding mental illness, during recent
years the massive publicity on this aspect of health has created
traumatic anxiety and concern in the thinking of many people.
This anxiety is due in part to a lack of understanding of the problem and also to the impression that mental illness requires long
years in a mental hospital or long expensive periods in the office
of a psychiatrist or psychoanalyst and this without an assured hope
of recovery.

Since there are no laboratory tests to identify mental illness, and
since the symptoms of this sickness are frequently obscured and
the expression of these symptoms often bizarre and strange, it will
be helpful and reassuring to state in general terms the characteristics of persons who experience normal mental and emotional
health.

What are some of the characteristics you expect to find in a
person with good mental health?

Keep in mind the fact that *people are different.* Nowhere in the
world will you find two persons who are exactly alike. Our bodies

are unique—each one in some way is unlike the other. From a physical aspect, the average or normal person is one who in a general way is not very different from the rest of us.

In looking for the person who has good mental health we find the same thing—*people are different.* They think and feel in their own individual way. Not only bodies, but minds are unique—each one unlike any other mind.

However, there are certain attitudes (habits of thinking and feeling) which, to a reasonable degree, are found in all normal people—those with good mental health.

1. You will find that a person with normal mental health is able to deal with the demands of life as they come. He does it by attacking the problems of the day as they arise. He knows that the problems of tomorrow cannot be solved by worrying about them today. This is a far different thing from planning new techniques or trying to avoid problems before they arise. There is a vast difference between planning and worrying. Utopian daydreaming does not solve problems. A person with normal mental health must face reality. Problems are never solved by running away from them. Challenge every new obstacle you meet, rather than yield to it. Give any situation all you have, then be satisfied when you reach your limit.

2. People with good mental health have at least one thing in common—they like themselves. You cannot be happy and do good work unless you have a good opinion of yourself. Good mental health and happiness are two sides of the same coin. This does not mean that you must have an inflated opinion of yourself. Nor does it mean that you are perfectly satisfied with yourself. It simply means that way down deep inside, you have a healthy approval of yourself. You cannot undersell yourself and do creative and satisfactory work. If you hate yourself (or anyone else) you limit your ability and may destroy your physical as well as your mental health. Love, in itself, is both dynamic and therapeutic.

The man with good mental health has emotions like anyone else, but they don't explode for little or no cause. When he gets mad, his anger is in proportion to what caused it. He doesn't fly off the handle for unimportant reasons. He experiences fear, love, hate, jealousy, guilt and worry—but he isn't overcome by any of them.

3. People who have good mental health accept their responsibilities. If the demands of life are too great or unfair, then they begin planned changes. And, when they discover that situations cannot be altered, they simply adjust to (accept) whatever is necessary. This "adjustment" is not a resignation with the same meaning as a defeat. It is, rather, a healthy facing of reality. If the adjustment that must be made is too severe, then they plan for a new work or start a long-range program to change their environment.

The person whose mental health is functioning in a normal manner expects to like and trust other people and assumes that they will like him. He is tolerant of the shortcomings of others just as he is of his own. He does not expect them to be perfect, either. He does not try to push people around and will not be pushed around himself. He is capable of loving other people and thinking about their interests and well-being. He has friendships that are satisfying and lasting.

4. Healthy-minded people plan for the future. They attempt to mold it to their own size. They do not know what will happen any more than anybody else does, but they do not fear the future. They have confidence that each new day will provide solutions for any problems they must consider. By planning for the future you can make your own destiny. Everything we have done, thought, and felt in the past makes us what we are today. In this way we build our personality and our station in our environment. What we will be and have in the future will be the result of our actions, thoughts, and feelings in the past and today. We get what we earn—no more and no less. It is a true fact of experience that you tend to become what your mind pictures, provided you give the mental picture strong emotional support, and if the objective is sound. You can reach your goal; your best dreams can come true. You can get to where you want to go, if you just know where it is. Many people get nowhere simply because they do not know where they want to go. This is true because we live in that kind of a world.

5. People who are healthy-minded are able to think for them-

selves. They make their own decisions and then accept the responsibility for making them. When they make mistakes, they acknowledge them. But instead of crying over them, they resolve never to make the same mistakes again. They are not like the person who makes the same mistakes over and over with the same unpleasant result. They profit by their mistakes.

6. To have mental health is to find a reasonable amount of happiness and satisfaction in your work and in day by day activities. Within your mind are all the resources needed for successful living. Unhappiness is an illness of the mind. Like tuberculosis, it is communicable; it is passed from one person to another. Like opium, it is habit-forming. Like all habits, it is self-induced; we think and feel what we want to think and feel. You are the boss of your mind.

Good mental health means that one can identify himself with a group, can feel that he is a part of it, and has a sense of responsibility to his neighbors and fellowman. He handles problems as they come up. He tries for goals he thinks he can achieve through his own abilities; he doesn't want the moon on a silver platter. He does whatever he undertakes to the best of his ability. If the result is not perfect, he does not fret about it but just tries to do better the next time. He enjoys his work.

7. Men and women who have normal mental health welcome change and new experiences. It is impossible to stand still. We are —whether we like it or not—always changing. The flesh and blood of our bodies change within a short period. We are always going forward or backward. Change is a definite part of life. The one essential thing in a normal person's life is his ability to adjust himself, without frustration and failure, to changing situations.

In the treatment of mental illness and the building of positive mental health, the basic character of the subconscious is perhaps the central concept of psychiatry. Man's character has been compared to an iceberg, seven-eighths of which is under water and unseen. Glimpses of subconscious power are found in dreams and fantasies, as well as the intuitions and insights which are used by all creative people, whether in medicine, the arts, or business. The subconscious is like a safe-deposit box in which we place pleasant or unpleasant thoughts, wholesome creative emotions as well as frustrations and anxieties. Some of these we attempt to forget, but these mental and emotional memories persist. Some of these memories can be recalled during periods of relaxation, but the greater part of such memories is buried deep within the subconscious. Since thoughts and emotions remain, they must be held within an area of the mind other than in conscious awareness.

The problem of maintaining good mental health grows out of the fact that the main stream of mental and emotional activity which we have experienced is not available to the conscious mind for analysis and evaluation. However, these buried experiences are not inert by any means. They are an active ingredient in the subconscious energy of our personality and, as such an active ingredient they discharge energy (thoughts and emotions) into the conscious part of mind. The problem is that the conscious part of mind is rarely, if ever, aware of this discharge of energy. It is conditioned without conscious awareness that the conditioning process has been accomplished.

The subconscious is often interpreted as though it were a special biological region of the brain. In point of fact, neither conscious nor subconscious mind is an anatomical entity. The term subconscious refers primarily to operations of the mind taking place without conscious recognition of these operations. Nevertheless the operation of mental processes beyond conscious awareness is increasingly regarded as a major problem for psychiatry, medicine and the behavioral sciences.

The subconscious activity involves a vast storehouse of everything we have experienced from the time of birth to the present. Each sensory perception, emotion, idea, judgment and reason is recorded in minute detail. Evidence of these experiences may be hidden and forgotten but they often emerge in moments of relaxation and more rarely in periods of stress. This part of our mind is always active, operating twenty-four hours a day. Regarding this emergence of childhood experiences, Dr. George Christian Anderson of The Academy of Religion and Mental Health, in an address, recently stated, "Early repressions often push through seeking expression like air bubbles from the dark mud in the lily pond." All the past events of our lives are an active part of our personality structure. It is utterly impossible to completely escape from the influence of our thoughts, words and deeds once we have felt or expressed them.

These considerations do not indicate that a person is a helpless puppet driven by subconscious instinctual desires and forces. The conscious mind, let it be stated again, controls and determines the content of the subconscious. Experiences, emotions, thoughts and anxieties placed in the subconscious can be neutralized and transformed by a persistent and continuing process of redirection by the conscious mind. Mental catalysts can be discharged by the conscious mind into the subconscious and thereby activate a reconditioning process which will neutralize, limit and, in many instances, expel all elements of previous traumatic mental and emotional activities.

14

THE MANAGEMENT OF FEAR AND ANXIETY

PERHAPS as a child you read the story of Gulliver and his visit to the Land of Laputa. The citizens of that ancient country lived in a state of constant anxiety and fear. Like many of our day, they never enjoyed a moment's peace of mind.

These people were afraid that the orderly movements of the sun and stars would be disrupted and bring destruction to all forms of life. Perhaps the earth would move too close to the sun and be reduced to molten lava. If this did not happen, certainly the energy of the sun would in the near future be exhausted and life would be made impossible by the intense cold which would fill all space. Surely there was imminent danger that the earth would be struck by the tail of a comet and reduced to ashes.

The difference between the people Gulliver found in Laputa and those of our modern age is found in the condition, or object, which brings about anxiety. The chorus of fear, from ancient Athens to the Bikini Atoll, is much the same. Our fears range all the way from the destruction of the earth by the atom bomb to losing our jobs and our health. The very structure of modern society is built on anxiety.

Despite the achievements of science and technology, we are a phobia-ridden people. All the Utopian fantasies of social planning and of scientific research will not remove these anxieties. They arise from within ourselves. It is from within ourselves that real security will be achieved. Centuries ago Seneca made the statement, "Fear makes a poison in the blood." It is an accepted data that fear and anxiety cause the physiologic processes of the human body to function abnormally. Not only the insight revealed by modern psychology and psychiatry but the day-to-day experience of people alike confirm the truth of this statement.

When a person experiences fear or anxiety, the body reacts in very much the way it does to anger. The heart increases its speed—the pulse is rapid. The small blood vessels contract, the skin tends to turn white, blood pressure is increased. The supply of blood to the stomach and intestines is transferred to the heart, lungs, the brain and skeletal muscles. The liver throws a new supply of sugar into the blood. The spleen supplies additional red blood cells. The muscles of the chest are relaxed, thus increasing the capacity of the air passages. The smooth muscles of the skin contract and conserve heat. If exposed to the air the blood coagulates more rapidly. Certain of the endocrine glands react. The adrenals discharge adrenalin into the blood in increased proportions. The thyroid gland speeds up all processes of the body by increasing one of its secretions, thyroxin.

All of these changes are automatic. They are not subject to conscious control.

Fear affects every normal process of the human body. Consider these statements by Dr. George W. Crile, a recognized authority in this field, "Fear influences every organ and tissue. . . ." "That the brain is influenced—damaged even—by fear has been proved." [1]

Fear prepares the body for immediate action—fight or flight. This action process is rarely possible in modern life. Thus, fear results in frustration and destroys the balance of the body's natural processes. Dr. Crile described the symptoms in animals at a time when they were stricken by sudden fear. "They may be likened to an automobile with the clutch thrown out but whose engine is racing

[1] George W. Crile, M.D., *The Origin and Nature of the Emotions* (New York: Saunders and Company).

at full speed. The gasoline is being consumed, and machinery is being worn; but the machine as a whole does not move, though the power of its engine may cause it to tremble."

Disease and health, like success and failure, are rooted in mental and emotional processes. Unhealthy thoughts will express themselves through a sickly body. Thousands of people are limited in health and efficiency and die prematurely because of fear, frustration, anxiety and worry. These emotions demoralize the whole body.

The body may suffer illness without the mind becoming ill. Seldom does the mind become sick without the body reflecting the illness in disease of one kind or another. The body is the servant of the mind.

Fear and hate, if continued over a period of years, may, and frequently do, produce incurable body deformities. A friend, who is a well-known physician, described a case which illustrates the situation. A man who came to a mental health clinic had for a number of years engaged in a bitter struggle with his son-in-law. The joints of his legs and arms were afflicted with what appeared to be arthritis. He called it rheumatism. All the various tests available to medical science showed no local infection of teeth or tonsils, the conditions which are often the cause of rheumatism and arthritis.

The trouble lay deeper. It was in his mental and emotional makeup. This man was a widower living with his two daughters, the eldest of whom was seeking a divorce and the custody of a child. The son-in-law had plenty of money and good lawyers. Every possible legal trick was used to delay a decision in the case.

As the patient told how he hated his son-in-law, he knotted and twisted his legs, arms and fingers with the frustrated motion of a person who would kick, bite or strangle an opponent. His frustration and hostility, reinforced by his fear of ultimate defeat, had extended to the muscles of his body. He had lived so long under the compulsion of fear and anxiety that he was permanently deformed.

Experiences and the emotions which are always an ingredient in any meaningful situation are embodied in us. When we try to drive them out of our minds, we often succeed only in banishing them to the subconscious part of our mind, from which area they are freer to create havoc than when they were in our conscious mind. The more forcefully we exclude them from self-awareness, the more readily are they pressed into the tissues of our body, appearing then as body sickness.

Alexis Carrel, who was known throughout the world as a scientist and physician, made this statement: "Thought can generate organic lesions. . . . Thus, envy, hate, fear, when these sentiments are habitual, are capable of starting organic changes and genuine diseases." [2]

The anxieties of modern man are such that they can seldom be solved by physical action. If a man is suffering anxiety and fear because he has just lost his job, he cannot give release to his emotion in any physical way that will remove the situation he is worrying about. But the physical mechanism he inherited from his caveman ancestors is still functioning just as it did in prehistoric times, and it pours various internal secretions into his bloodstream which are not worked off by action. It is now recognized that all the physiological processes of the human body, especially the activity of the glands of internal secretion respond to mental and emotional stimuli. Without action immediately following, this response to mental and emotional stimuli may load the human body with substances which are not needed and which may, therefore, be as harmful as disease germs. While this poisoning effect is expressed through a biochemical process, the inciting cause is found in psychic impulses.

The processes of digestion and assimilation are controlled by the subconscious part of the mind by way of the autonomic nervous system. This, of course, is without conscious effort on the part of the individual. If the digestive organism is prevented from functioning in a normal way by fear, anger, frustration, in fact, by any disturbing emotion, incomplete digestion results. This means poor assimilation. Incomplete assimilation means inadequate nutrition.

[2] Alexis Carrel, *Man, The Unknown* (New York: Harper & Row, Publishers).

This deficiency results in debilitated nerve energy; this, in turn, means little energy for endurance and efficient work. The result is that the body is susceptible to disease; to many petty irritations, worries, angers, disappointments; and to general inefficiency and despair. Thus the unwholesome cycle perpetuates itself. Mental and emotional disturbances engender digestive trouble, which in turn makes the sufferer more susceptible to mental and emotional disturbances. Stomach trouble ordinarily is the result, not the cause, of mental and emotional disturbances. Mental and emotional tone and color are just as important to good health as are the food elements. It is true that digestive and assimilative processes are largely automatic—they are run by the subconscious mind. It should also be remembered that the subconscious receives its direction, its point of view, its tone, its color and its efficiency from the conscious mind.

The conclusion of the whole matter is that the mind is the controlling force in the process of digestion, and that any person who does not keep his mind toned up may find indigestion ruining his efficiency and destroying the whole plan and scope of his life.

Fear, like Mary Shelley's Frankenstein, must be destroyed before it destroys us, its creators.

In facing the problem of fear and anxiety, the first step is to think out and form a constructive philosophy of life. By this is meant not some vague, intellectual idea about life and the Universe, but a standard by which the value or worth of any thing or any condition may be determined.

Whatever good or ill fortune any situation holds for you depends not so much on the situation in itself, but on you—on your attitude of intelligent faith, courage and understanding; or upon your surrender to fear and anxiety, followed by hysteria and panic. Everyone has observed two people experiencing the same troubles. One of the two is overwhelmed and utterly defeated; the other finds in the same condition a stimulus for courageous work and great achievement. One is the helpless pawn of circumstances, of events; the other has a long-range constructive philosophy of life.

Because of the nature of reality we think and feel whatever we desire to think and feel. Every person's life is self-starting and self-going. We ourselves decide where we want to go, and we also determine the mode of travel and largely the condition of the road over which we will travel. Since each individual is self-starting and self-directing, we actually create fear, worry and anxiety. Every fear, every anxiety is self-induced; the emotion and fear and anxiety (as is true of every thought or feeling) comes from within. It makes no difference what causes one to fear—the menace of atomic destruction, the danger of losing one's job, the threat of sickness— the reason why we fear is the same. We fear because we want to fear. We indulge ourselves.

The normal purpose of fear is to prepare the body or mind for action—appropriate action to take care of the situation. Fear is harmful only when action does not result. Anxiety, the feeling that there is no way out, is the result of fear without the release of action.

Since the basic assumption of a sound, long-range philosophy of life has already been stated, it is only necessary to recall again the twofold nature of mind. Each of us individually is conscious and subconscious mind. Through the conscious aspect of mind, we reason, discriminate, decide upon methods and objectives—in short, we determine the how and where of the journey of life. In the subconscious aspect of mind we have available power and insight which, when properly used, will create for us anything we want.

In dealing with fear and anxiety, the conscious mind must investigate, find all the facts, analyze their meaning and bearing. This is the modern form of action, replacing the brute physical action of the cave man. It is mental rather than physical activity.

In the light of this mental activity, the conscious mind must decide the attitude which we are to take regarding any disturbing situation. When this is done, the problem can be turned over to the subconscious aspect of the mind with instructions to find a way out.

Consider the following practical—and psychologically sound— suggestions for conquering fear, worry and frustration:

1. The first principle for relieving and curing the emotion of fear or anxiety is to face honestly and couragesouly the fact of the fear

itself. Nothing can be accomplished by ignoring or repressing a state of fear. Amnesia is not a cure for fear. Face the fact of fear and its cause. This is the foundation for the mastery of the emotion of fear.

Facing fear courageously often helps us to discover that its danger and threat have been overrated. John Masefield, the English poet, pictures this fact in his poem called "The Hell-Hounds." Withiel, the hero of the tale, is pursued by fears which the poet thinks of as hounds in the hunt. He runs until his strength is exhausted. He can go no farther. In desperation he turns about and faces his pursuers. He discovers then that the powerful hounds which have seemed ready to destroy him have been transformed, as if by magic, into a feeble and lifeless form which can easily be overpowered.

2. Don't expect the worst. It seldom happens. It does no good to carry around a lightning rod to attract trouble. Most of our fears of the unexpected do not materialize. For example, for many years the common cactus plant was regarded as one of the threats to mankind. The destruction of rich and fertile lands by this stubborn weed was believed inevitable. Many saw a tragic future for whole sections of the country as the lowly cactus continued to push forward.

These dire predictions of disaster did not come about! Instead, this plant has become a large source of revenue for thousands of people. Fifty years ago the cactus seemed to offer nothing to mankind except a barrier to progress. All the fear of the unexpected could have been avoided by facing the future with high courage and the perspective of faith.

3. Accept the fact that you are afraid. Then ˄ssemble all the facts about the situation which are causing you to experience fear, anxiety or frustration. Look these facts straight in the face. Is there anything you can do to solve the problem? If there is, act at once with confidence and enthusiasm. Make your decision. Act upon it, and then quit thinking about it. Don't stew in your own juice. Emerson was right when he said, "Do the thing you fear and the death of fear is certain." Worry and frustration are a "circle of inefficient thought whirling about a pivot of fear." The instant you

pin down a fear by intelligent action, you are on the way to a solution.

Fear, or anxiety, is an emotion within the person. You cannot escape your shadow on a moonlight night. The fear, or anxiety, is a part of your inner mental life. To live continuously with thoughts of fear, cynicism, suspicion and worry is to be confined in a self-made prison.

To fear disease, failure or trouble is to sow seeds in the subconscious mind that will bring forth a harvest of ill health, confused mental states and misdirected actions in mind and body.

The more intense the fear, the deeper the subconscious impression and the more we shall receive of that which we feared. "That which I have greatly feared has come upon me."

4. A change of climate, or a vacation, or a different kind of work will do little, if any, good. You must deal with yourself. Your problem is written; face the facts; then reverse your thinking.

For example, take the case of Bill Jones. This man for a number of years was a successful member of a well-known advertising firm. He lost his position through no fault of his own—a rearrangement of the membership of the firm which he could not influence or control. After a few months he secured another position. It was not as good as the one he lost, but the salary was fair and the chance for advancement good. Somehow Bill Jones could not forget his ill-fortune. The loss of his previous job was a sore spot in his life. Resentment and brooding became habitual. His inner poise was destroyed; his efficiency dropped. His health became impaired. The wholesome emotional balance which formerly supported his efforts was lost.

It was not the loss of the job which destroyed his opportunity for future happiness and the chance for advancement in the new position. Bill Jones limited himself by his resentment and lack of appreciation. Whatever a man sows in thought and feeling he will reap in experience. Life as we experience it is an authentic reflection of our mental and emotional activity.

5. It is true that a certain amount of fear is a constructive influence in the life of the individual or the race. It leads to alertness

and effort for self-improvement. One of the basic chemical reactions of the body, that of the adrenal glands, provides power for rapid movement in the presence of fear or danger. Shakespeare has Laertes remind Ophelia that "safety lies in fear." It is an observation which is valid in every age. Recognize this fact for its full value. Use it to produce positive mental action.

6. As in all other aspects of life, avoid the habit of fear. Do not allow dread, or anxiety, or worry to become fixed as a mental or emotional habit. Enlist your subconscious mind in a campaign of positive, constructive, happy thoughts or ideas.

It is highly important that attitudes of suspicion and jealousy not be entertained. It is impossible to expel fear when the mind is filled with jealousy, suspicion, irritation and negative thinking. Fear destroys hope and expectancy. Here again direct your subconscious mind to divert your emotions into pleasant, tolerant, confident channels.

The period just before going to sleep is perhaps the most important hour of the day. Never go to sleep discouraged, nor with the thought of failure or anxiety in mind. To fear failure while going to sleep is to impress the subconscious with the idea of failure, and the subconscious must respond by producing conditions that reflect your conscious thoughts.

The subconscious mind is somewhat similar to a phonograph; it records everything you think and feel. There is this difference, however. The subconscious not only reproduces exactly what has been recorded, but will also form, create, develop and express the full potential of what your mind desired when the impression was made.

7. It is important to recognize that the physical world as well as the social world is held together by the constructive emotions. Fear is disintegrating. The positive emotions are cohesive; they hold together, build up and construct. An attitude of good will toward the thing, condition, or person feared will rob an "anxiety state" of its terror. There is a fundamental law of mind which may be stated in three words, "Like perceives like." One sees other persons, things and conditions through the color of his own mental and

emotional makeup. Recall the words of the French psysicist, Marie Curie: "Nothing in life is to be feared. It is only to be understood."

8. Have faith in yourself and the Universe. Don't worry too much about what lies ahead. Go as far as you can see, and when you get there more light will be available. The cause of failure is not so much the load we are carrying now, but the weight of what we fear may be tomorrow's burden. There is an old Bulgarian proverb that expresses an insight that has grown out of centuries of human experience, "God promises a safe landing, but not a calm passage." In many instances lack of faith is man's greatest enemy and the road block that limits his progress.

All of these suggestions, and everything that has been said about anxiety and fear, applies also to frustration, that ever-present, modern-day phenomenon. Frustration, which in most instances is an end-result of fear, probably causes more physical ailments than all the microbes in creation. All the pills in the corner drugstore cannot cure a person whose life is beset by fear and anxiety. It can spoil our days and poison our lives. We must face it and conquer it—or it will conquer us.

Faith and fear determine the color, tone and content of our mental activity. Fear destroys the creative power of our minds. The end-result of fear is mental and emotional myopia. On the other hand, faith steadies the imagination. Chronic fear and anxiety are a mental blight, a moral mildew, and an intellectual poison. Long ago, Pythagoras said, "Fear makes a poison in the blood."

Fear, anxiety and worry can be conquered, effectively removed from your life, by recognizing the power of your subconscious mind when properly directed. You can and do build the house in which you live.

15

THE OTHER SIDE
OF THE
FREUDIAN COIN

AMONG sophisticated Americans perhaps no word tends to create anxiety and fear as much as the use of Freud's term, "the unconscious." As mentioned in a previous chapter, Freud's illustrative analogy of the human mind as being like an iceberg nine-tenths below and one-tenth above the surface of the water indicates (correctly) that the human personality is largely controlled and its expression determined by the underlying basic part of the mind. Unfortunately, this analogy also tends to create the impression that the conscious part of the mind (the one-tenth above the level of the water) is automatically and inescapably controlled by the submerged part.

Since the emergence of psychiatry as a medical discipline, the subconscious (unconscious) has been associated with abnormal and traumatic mental episodes. In addition, it has been recognized as the cause of deviant and antisocial behavior patterns. This association of the subconscious with so-called instinctual drives, the lodging place of limiting complexes, has all but destroyed in the average person any conviction that he can direct his own life and determine the content and expression of his experience.

The first fact to be stated, is that the subconscious is not a reservoir of energy like a menacing demon whose sole purpose is to

create misery and abnormalities. As a matter of every day experience, the subconscious must be regarded as a person's guardian
angel—*if* it is correctly directed by the conscious mind. If there are
demons, they are found in the work of the conscious mind and in
the direction which it imposes upon the subconscious.

Many people have come to regard the subconscious as a dangerous, ghastly pool of energy which expresses itself in paralysis, in
inhibitions and in road blocks to the desired development of one's
life. The activity of the submerged part of the mind reflects the
desires of the conscious mind. This fact should be recognized, since
every horrible traumatic experience—from unwholesome dreams, to
Fascism in recent literature—has been explained as the workings
of the subconscious. "The unconscious is a friendly companion
and, if treated like a friend, it can be your best and most helpful
ally; an inexhaustible source of elation and deep satisfaction, of
hidden delights and manifest accomplishments." [1]

Notwithstanding the massive psychiatric literature which pictures
the subconscious as filled exclusively with complicated traumatic
and barbaric drives, the subconscious is certainly the reservoir of
humane, wholesome feelings and attitudes. The subconscious part
of our personality can be transformed into a constant source of
creative energy, of elation and inner contentment, and into a recovering process against disease and failure. Viewed objectively,
the subconscious is a source of light, of high intuition and of creative insight.

Do not be afraid of the submerged area of your mind. Your living, creative subconscious is, of course, the repository of all your
mental and emotional activity; whether that activity be good or bad,
normal or abnormal, it is also a source of renewing strength and
rebuilding power which controls your life.

Every thoughtful investigator immediately recognizes the fact
that the subconscious mind, as it expresses itself in the life of the
average person, contains a gold mine as well as a "rubbish dump."
However, a fact equally significant is seldom understood. The orig-

[1] Stephan Lackner, M.D., *Discover Your Self* (New York: Fawcett World
Library).

inal endowment of the underlying part of the mind is uncondi-
tioned mental and emotional energy. This reservoir of energy is
neutral and impersonal. It is the willing servant of the volitional
self-aware aspect of mind. The conscious mind corresponds to the
navigator of a modern ship who determines the direction, the speed
and the destination of his vessel. The subconscious area of mind is
similar to the massive apparatus which carries the navigator and his
cargo to its appointed destination.

The content of the subconscious mind, whether it be that of a
gold mine or a rubbish dump, is due entirely and completely to the
mental and emotional processes of the conscious mind. Its tone,
color and dynamics are not due to activity originating within itself,
but reflect obediently and completely the aim and purposes of the
higher level of mind.

The long history of subconscious intuition and inspiration, which
is chiefly responsible for the intellectual progress of the human
race, provides significant evidence that the human mind extends
far beyond the conscious boundary in a positive direction. Whether
subconscious activity is directed in a positive, constructive way, or
channeled in negative, trauma-producing action, depends upon the
direction or charge placed into it by the conscious mind.

Every creative thinker receives his basic ideas from outside his
conscious mind. Poets, authors, musicians and scientists acknowledge that their greatest work is due to insight not received or
formulated by the conscious mind, but arising from the submerged
area of personality. Every person with the quality known as "genius" is an example of subconscious mentation.

The basic drive or motivation of the human personality as described by Freud may be stated as the "pleasure principle," or the
"will to pleasure." This "will to pleasure" seeks the uninhibited
flow of certain instinctual energies, especially those of sex and aggression. In Freud's thinking, the subconscious is a region of the
mind which is absolutely impersonal and which operates as a machine and functions without constructive energy in determining
the experience or attitude of a person.

Under this concept it is assumed that the subconscious (unconscious) is influenced only by thoughts and feelings of hate, aggression and by impulses resulting from inhibited or unused sexual energy.

In the Freudian concept, the individual is but the helpless pawn of the unconscious instinctual energies and drives within himself. The individual is not only incapable of self-direction and reeducation, but the individual should not blame or punish himself for any act. As one understanding psychologist has recently said in referring to the Freudian viewpoint, "We should love and accept and respect ourselves perfectly and so completely and so unconditionally that we refuse to condemn, punish or 'tramp on' ourselves, no matter what! This, I submit, is not self-respect. This is the ultimate in self-contempt and rejection! For it requires us to regard ourselves, not as human beings, but as a variety of organism not basically different from the beasts of field and jungle, with no morality, no standards, no character, no spirit. Who wants to lose this capacity to condemn and punish himself if he really behaves badly?" [2]

As a code of conduct for the individual or group, the Freudian concept is entirely negative. Its sentiments and attitudes regarding man's capability would, if applied literally, prevent the individual from attempting anything positive and certainly renders him unable to develop anything new. This is indicated by the terminology frequently used by those who adhere to the freudian concept. There is repeated reference to personal insecurity, instability, frustration, trauma and tensions. Still more significant is the complete absence in Freudian literature of such terms as self-confidence, personal integrity, self-reliance, or the idea of personal responsibility.

In its total meaning, the Freudian concept assumes that human beings cannot be responsible for anything; we are all helpless cogs in a vast cause-and-effect complex and are in no way accountable for what we are, or for that matter, for anything that occurs in our experience. Certainly there is no empirical, much less scientific, justification for this assumption.

It seems to be a common trait for human beings to welcome any

[2] O. Hobart Mowrer, *The Crisis in Psychiatry and Religion* (Princeton, N.J.: D. Van Nostrand Co., Inc.). Used by permission.

idea that relieves them of responsibility for their failures or frustrations. Many people look on the subconscious as a sort of deeply buried vault full of malice and hostility and uncontrollable sex energy. The truth is that the subconscious mind is the most basic element of personality. Without the ever-active energy and creative power of the subconscious, human experience would be a mass of frustration and confusion. Certainly the subconscious is not simply a storehouse for the unhappy experience of life. Just as we have developed good and bad habits of thinking and acting, so we have formed good and bad memories that form a part of the energies of the subconscious.

The response of the individual to any situation is the fact that is significant. Environment, be it favorable or unfavorable, is but the reflection of one's thinking processes—the creation of his own hell or heaven through the action of his own mind.

One of the outstanding psychiatrist physicians of the nation, Dr. Leon J. Saul, has an important statement regarding the nature of the underlying reality of personality: "The id, quite naturally, generates mature drives, as well as those which are immature and those which are of a basic nature and not properly classifiable as mature or immature. By 'immature' is meant the drives and the responses of the organism before it reaches its full growth and full adult powers. The circulation of the infant before birth differs from that after birth. The babe suckles and is parasitically dependent upon the mother. But when it reaches adulthood it is driven by desires for independence, for mating, for home and offspring, as is seen throughout the animal kingdom. Many lower species furnish fine examples of diligent nesting, parenthood and fidelity, as well as of alert, conscientious, productive work. Go not only to the ants, but to the great felines, the gibbons, the birds and even to your pets, if their id-drives are not too corrupted by domestication. This is pointed out because not uncommonly the id is spoken of as though it generated only infantile urges, whereas obviously the mature drives of the adult also well up from the id." [3]

[3] Leon J. Saul, M.D., *The Bases of Human Behavior* (Philadelphia: J. B. Lippincott Co.). Used by permission.

Dr. William Brown, the world famous British psychiatrist, has a revealing statement in one of his books regarding the ability of the average person to achieve redirection and self-control in his experience:

> I should like, in conclusion, to emphasize the value and importance of formal suggestion and autosuggestion for the normal person as a means of increasing his mental powers in various directions. If he makes calm affirmations to himself while lying on a couch in a state of mental and muscular relaxation, such affirmations may be realized by subconscious mental activity and in this way he may improve his powers of mental concentration, his memory, and his mental aptitude along special lines. He may also correct bad habits and increase self-confidence and self-control. Often suggestion treatment from another person is needed to give him a start, and then he can carry on by himself.

In the course of his medical practice, Freud found that certain thoughts drop out of the normal consciousness of the individual and go on working underground. Although these thoughts are repressed from the self-awareness of the individual, they continue to exist and to influence conduct. To repressed thoughts of this kind, active beyond the reach of voluntary recall, he gave the name "unconscious." To those thoughts which, although ordinarily outside normal consciousness, can be recalled at times by voluntary effort was given the name "preconscious."

Due to the fact that Freud was dealing with mentally sick people, he gave little thought and consideration to experience and data regarding the functioning of the normal mind. Certainly it is true that some thoughts are so utterly disagreeable and so completely contradict the normal standards of conduct that they are rejected by the conscious mind and thus deposited in the subconscious. This is only half of the picture. Every thought, every feeling and every aspiration experienced by an individual becomes a part of the subconscious mind. To assume that only those thoughts which are unacceptable are deposited in the subconscious mind is to state a conclusion that is contradicted by the everyday experience of normal people. The subconscious mind is not simply a reservoir of trauma, of frustration and guilt; it is also a sustaining repository of every creative impulse, of every integrating, constructive thought or emotion held by the individual. The conscious and subconscious are not separate and distinct areas of activity. They represent a unified process by which the mental and emotional health and the creative ability of each individual is developed.

One difficulty with Freudian thinking is that it is based too largely on selected data. To develop a messianic complex and attempt to create a moral and social revolution, based simply on a study of the way the minds of a limited number of sick people function, is to stray away from the intellectual ideal of that outstanding physicist, Lord Kelvin, when he said, "Science is bound by the everlasting law of honor to face fearlessly every problem which can be fairly presented to it." Certainly this requires the consideration of all available data before attempting to formulate a general conclusion. To again quote Dr. Saul: "The basic pattern of each individual's personality is generally remote from consciousness, yet this 'nuclear emotional constellation' determines the ways in which we all live our lives. Unconscious emotional forces and mental processes not only generate symptoms but dominate lives." [4]

If the insight of this outstanding psychiatrist physician is adequately expressed, the function of the subconscious (unconscious) is not simply and only to act as host to unhealthy traumatic concepts and feelings, but it is also the energy or directing force which "determines the ways in which we all live our lives."

Another equally eminent psychiatrist, Dr. William S. Sadler, has this statement: "The power of the subconscious is profound, sublime, and almost unbelievable. To summarize the province of the subconscious would be to enumerate all the emotional and intellectual phenomena of human experience." [5]

Unless the concept of a self-directing creative mind is utterly false, we must accept the conclusion that peace of mind and health of body are self-bestowed and that failure, frustration and trouble

[4] Saul, *op. cit.*
[5] Wm. S. Sadler, M.D. and Lena K. Sadler, M.D., *Truth About Mental Healing* (Chicago: Follett Publishing Company). Used by permission.

are self-inflicted. Whether we understand fully the inner workings of the human mind or not, thoughts will continue to bind and free, inspire, degrade, achieve success, or produce failure, because the impact of events set in motion by the energy of mind is unavoidable. Our ability to select and control our thoughts is an inalienable human right too lightly stressed.

Practical human experience makes the assumption necessary and inescapable that whatever man can conceive, he can achieve; that whatever the mind of man can do, man's mind can undo; and that whatever mind can cure, mind can prevent.

16
CHILDHOOD TRAUMA AND SUBCONSCIOUS ACTIVITY

TO an extent that we seldom realize, many of us are imprisoned to a greater or lesser degree by our childhood. Like the unseen strings that control the movements of a marionette, we respond to long forgotten childhood experiences and memories, seldom, if ever, giving thought to what makes us act the way we do.

Here is a story of a mind that traveled far, but which, because of an experience in early childhood, imprisoned his body by chains stronger than steel.

This person was no ordinary man. He was a full professor in one of our great American universities. His mind was brilliant and his physical body was perfect, yet he was imprisoned by abject fear and terror within the limits of four or five city blocks. Not just for a short time, but for many years. Notwithstanding its imprisonment, this man's mind held the learning of thirty centuries and the mastery of a dozen ancient and modern languages. Great intellectual power and perfect physical health are not a barrier to the emotion of fear.

The imprisonment of this man started around 1910. While walking one afternoon he suddenly came face to face with a large billboard showing a locomotive rushing head on. He collapsed. That summer the thought of going more than a short distance from home turned his hair snow white. After long and exhaustive search with professional help, he found the source of his trouble. One day he recalled standing by the side of a railroad track when with a terrific roar a locomotive suddenly appeared like a nightmare beast intent on devouring him. After a great deal of work and investigation he was able to identify the occasion. In his mother's diary he finally discovered the date of this childhood experience which occurred when an onrushing locomotive almost caused his death and that of his mother. He was two years, four months, and ten days old at the time.

Thus he found the cause of his terror of locomotives and his fear of travel—the source of his life-long mental torture. By uncovering and understanding this buried childhood experience, he regained his poise and balance. His life became normal.

Instances of this kind occur by the thousands, perhaps not so dramatic, but nonetheless destructive in the building of a normal and useful life.

An instance of enslavement to a childhood experience is the case of acrophobia (fear of high places) which made life miserable for a twenty-one-year-old expectant mother of Los Angeles.

She and her husband lived on the tenth floor of a modern apartment house. This young woman (we will call her Anne), known to millions because of her work as a motion picture star, developed an hysterical terror of her lofty home. She begged her husband to find another place to live, lest she should not be able to resist the impulse to throw herself from the window.

In Los Angeles there is a high hill, called "The Angel's Flight" which used to be scaled by a long and very steep cable car. One evening when she was already in the car at the foot of the hill with her husband and two friends, about to be drawn up the incline, the remark of one of the friends caused her to glance up to the pavilion which was brightly lighted and high at the top of the track. She promptly fainted with a scream of terror. She had to be taken off the car and to a hospital. It was hours before she could be revived.

It is the theory of psychoanalysts that if a childhood memory is purposely forgotten, repressed, they say, the thing to do is to recall it, bring it into the conscious mind, then the trouble will be more likely to disappear.

When Anne was three years of age, a Mexican nursemaid had foolishly taken her for a ride on a Ferris wheel at an amusement park. Something went wrong with the mechanism, and the gondola in which the child and the nursemaid were riding was stuck for some twenty-five minutes at the top of the revolution. The child's terror at the long involuntary captivity at a great height threw her into a terrific panic. Her fear of high places from that time on made her life a nightmare. Months of exploratory work were required before she secured release from the impact of that childhood experience.

A less dramatic situation is that of Bill and his indigestion. The cause of Bill's indigestion goes back to his childhood. He was an only child. His mother was "bossy" and protected him too much. Bill turns all his attention upon himself. Other men think of their jobs or their families. Bill is interested only in himself. Of course, he feels unhappy and frustrated. This conflict inside himself comes out in the form of nervous indigestion.

Frequently men and women are imprisoned by some childhood mistake, a fancied wrong or slight, an accident, a fright; some by a story they read o were told which overimpressed their sensitive minds; some by ar experience with an unpleasant or cruel teacher, neighbor, relative or early employer, still others by mistakes in early sex educa'icn or experience and others by a horrible picture photographed on their memories

They are ..terally imprisoned by these childhood incidents or impressions these experiences are held n the self-aware area of thei mind they tend to dwell on them when they are weary or discouraged. They use them to excuse themselves for their weaknesses and failures. All their lives they autosuggest themselves into an attitude of resentment, self-depreciation, frustration, unhappiness, intolerance, fear, even failure. Such people have literally locked themselves in prisons of their own building, and have denied themselves the happiness and success that might be theirs.

How can any of us tell whether we are our own prisoners? There are four tests:

1. Do we find ourselves telling people of unhappy incidents, experiences or fears of our childhood?

2. Do we find ourselves dwelling mentally on our childhood years in a self-pitying way?

3. Do we excuse ourselves for a present failure or shortcoming by blaming something that happened in our childhood?

4. Do we feel envious and resentful of those who are surpassing us in achievement? Is there a continuing anxiety that successful work cannot be accomplished? Is there within us a compulsive drive to act differently in a particular situation from the way people ordinarily act?

The first step is to recognize the fact of your imprisonment. Having done this, alert yourself whenever your mind returns to a childhood wrong or fear and remind yourself that your prison door has no lock. Evaluate in a practical, realistic way your childhood experiences. Understanding and analysis will help to bring release.

1. The best thing to do is to look carefully within your own mind for attitudes and experiences which may be causing difficulties in your relations with other people. Early home experiences of jealousy, frequently within the family circle, may result in jealousy of fellow workers. It may be that authority in the home and school was so exercised as to create subconscious resentment toward necessary authority relating to your job. It is known that experiences of this kind may create attitudes that prevent promotion, or which even cause a man to quit his own job or get fired. People who cannot take orders rarely go very far in their work.

It is very important to recognize the source or cause of our attitude and reactions and to accept our own responsibility in these matters. It is not a particular experience that counts so much as the way we accept and evaluate that experience. We never come to a complete standstill in our progress until we place the responsibility for failure upon someone else.

2. Study again the four tests which may help you to determine the extent of your imprisonment by childhood experiences. Find some understanding person, a minister, priest, or physician, and talk with him honestly about how you feel. The mere fact of bringing an experience out into the open, putting it into words, will frequently bring understanding and release from its influence. The important thing about understanding childhood experiences is that they effect our feeling about ourselves as persons. They create lack of self-confidence, feelings of guilt, and this frequently results in one's acting out what he feels he is.

3. Accept honestly the changes in your feelings which follow honest expression and description of them. It is in this process that the rebuilding of personality is achieved. To understand an experience means that you will never condemn either yourself or others. Hostility and resentment constitute a terrible prison, the door of which can be opened by understanding and goodwill.

4. Realize that you can grow in your understanding and in the control of your emotions as long as you live. When one is growing he is never unhappy. Face forward and step out into the future without another minute's concern about your childhood. Your past is dead—bury it!

A word of caution: The average parent does not know, or fails to appreciate the fact, that a child's first mental and emotional equipment is basically subconscious mind and that the conscious mind is still in the process of development. The further assumption is made that spoken words and routine of care constitute the only avenue by which the child is impressed, and the very foundation of his future life is formed. That the child comes into the world with a tremendous reservoir of sensitive and unmotivated subconscious energy is seldom considered. The most important insight that has emerged from psychiatry and psychology is the fact that the future attitude, ability and response is largely formed in the very early months and years of the child's life. During this period when verbal communication is limited, the feelings, attitudes and unverbalized emotions of the parents (to a lesser extent of other people) are imprinted in the very fabric of the child's subconscious mind. That emotions and attitudes are communicated to the infant mind is a matter of common observation, as well as the proven insight of psychology.

It is true that "emotional forces control our lives" and this is preeminently true of the impressions received and retained by the young child. It is at this point that parents fail to realize that unknowingly they communicate to their child their own emotions, attitudes and thoughts. True the child cannot make a verbal response to these communicated emotions and unspoken thoughts, but a response is made in terms of the child's health, its attitude toward food and other routines connected with his developing body. The emotional forces implanted unknowingly by parents in the child's subconscious mind, condition, color and determine its response not only during infancy and young childhood but through the whole of its adult life.

Discord and unhappiness in the home, resentment, even when unspoken, of one parent toward another, the emotional attitude of parents toward other people are all involuntarily received by the child's subconscious mind and will later be expressed, if not corrected, in physical ill health, delinquency and other forms of limitations and, possibly, antisocial behavior.

One very effective way of dealing with problems which arise, first of all, would be to realize that all behavior is goal-seeking, that the child is attempting to find satisfaction, even though his efforts are disturbing.

Since the subconscious mind is the creative basic part of a child's endowment, efforts should be made to communicate with this part of the child's mind, imprinting upon its sensitive structure, ideas and thoughts of a wholesome nature. The fact that a child's mind can be impressed by repetition of thought during sleep has been abundantly established by the use of tape recordings and other similar instruments. Such methods, however, lack the emotional strength which can be established only by direct communication between the parent's mind and the child's subconscious mind.

One fortunate element in any situation involving a child is the fact that the subconscious energy of the child has not yet been conditioned strongly by the child's own conscious mind or by the minds of other people. In the early months and years the subconscious mind of a child is much like the unused pages of a copy book—still blank and waiting to be filled in. Since it is the nature of the subconscious to create and sustain the ideas received from the conscious mind, the retaining and remotivation of the child can be accomplished with less effort and more immediate results than at any other time in his life.

The closely-knit family unit of a previous generation is gone, perhaps forever. Many well-intended parents have no anchor to hold them steady in times of difficulty. That many break under the stress and strain of modern living is not surprising.

There is, however, a method by which the inner struggles and environmental difficulties can be controlled. This method consists in building strength and balance within the minds and emotions of the individual. The oft-repeated statement that each individual carves out his own destiny is an inescapable fact. The content of experience—destiny—is determined by the way the basic subconscious part of mind is used and directed. This is true because in this area is found the creative energy of the individual.

Many experiences, especially those occurring in early childhood, are completely repressed. They are buried deep in the submerged recesses of the subconscious mind, completely beyond recall by the conscious mind. Experiences, thoughts and feelings that are repressed, are certainly not inactive. A fact, experience, or situation, repressed to the deep areas of the subconscious are far more powerful than the memory of such experiences or attitudes would be in the conscious mind.

Since the subconscious is creative and dynamic, the power of any idea or experience placed in it is accelerated and enhanced. The repressed idea or experience is an active force which makes its impact upon every physiologic and intellectual process of the person. If the experience, or thought, that is repressed is unpleasant or threatening, the conscious mind continues to reject its emergence into the self-aware area of life. The most traumatic contents of the subconscious rarely, if ever, are allowed to emerge into the conscious part of the mind.

It is, however, the completely repressed experiences that constitute the most difficult and dynamic problems with which the individual and the psychiatrist must deal. It is estimated by some authorities that psychoanalysis can benefit and in some cases bring about complete recovery for about 60 per cent of the people having these treatments. This form of treatment is not available to everyone. In many areas of the country psychiatrists and psychoanalysts are few in number and their schedules are full for weeks or months in advance. Psychiatric treatment is long and because of this fact it is quite expensive.

There are methods, however, which if applied consistently and intelligently, bring relief and recovery from the impact of these repressed emotions and complexes to a majority of those applying this method.

Recall the process of catalysis. A catalyst placed in a given substance will change the nature of that element while the catalytic agent remains practically unchanged. There are also vaccines and serums, which when placed within the human body, modify its process and cause the manufacture of antibodies which protect against certain diseases.

In a somewhat similar manner there are mental catalysts, which when placed in the subconscious mind empowered by expectancy and emotional drive, will change and modify the content of subconscious energy and its expression.

If a person finds unfavorable and limiting conditions in his personality structure, and if these conditions are analyzed by the conscious mind as fully as possible, then the conscious mind can send down into the subconscious mental catalysts that will modify and change the activity of the subconscious and in this way dissolve the activity of the repressed traumatic experience. For example, some individuals experience anxiety and are fear-ridden. They suffer from a continuing feeling of insecurity and dread.

Since this atmosphere of anxiety and fear is the product of some experience repressed in the subconscious, the planting of mental catalysts involving the idea of courage, security and confidence will, if these mental catalysts are honestly and sincerely accepted by the intellect, dissolve, modify and recreate activity and power in the subconscious which will relieve the situation.

Consider the person who lacks confidence in himself—one who is described as having an "inferiority complex." This person can, if he so desires, by a realistic evaluation of the facts of life, build into his personality the elements of self-confidence, courage and achievement. Admittedly, this is not a quick or easy process. The rebuilding of personality requires the sustained action of the volitional area of the mind empowered by faith and expectancy. In the thinking of many people, the rebuilding and redirecting of a personality that is experienced in religious conversion is accomplished by this process. Certainly the cosmic mind is biased in favor of the full development of the human potential rather than a condition of deterioration and failure.

The life of the human personality can remold and redirect itself and thus cause the physiologic condition of the human body and the environment in which the human personality is placed to reflect back to the person what he wants himself to be and the conditions under which he desires to live.

Illness caused by mental and emotional activity can be relieved by mind. Since illnesses and limitations due to repression are caused by unhealthy mental processes, the effect can be changed by changing the cause. Read again the chapter on Autosuggestion.

17

THE DIMENSIONS
OF MIND

IN our present intellectual climate, if one is to consider adequately the dimensions of mind, it is important not to adopt the position of the learned professor of Padua who refused to look through Galileo's telescope. He was afraid he would see what he did not wish to see and that the revelation of the new instrument would disturb his basic assumption regarding man and his place in the Universe. He failed to remember that what we prefer, like or dislike, in no way alters the reality of a situation.

This study makes the assumption with Cudworth that mind is "senior to the world and the architect thereof." Mind activity is at least a present factor in the scheme of nature, and it is by mind activity alone that nature can be studied and evaluated. The vast and imposing array of scientific facts, observations and concepts are but the findings of the mind. The primacy of mind consists simply in this fact: All aspects of reality must be submitted for its judgment and evaluation. The concept of the Cosmos as intelligent and purposeful has no other assurance.

To explain mind as arising out of the elements of the world it reveals, is to say that the mirror is constructed out of the objects it reflects. In this viewpoint you ascribe the origin of consciousness to the elements which bring it to light. You say that the knower emerges out of what he knows, the discoverer of the scenery out of the scenery which he discovers. In this case, if there were no observing mind, there would be in effect no scenery and no world; for the world has no knowledge of itself.

Our viewpoint is certainly limited if we imagine that our five senses encompass the Universe, or that our present understanding reveals its many aspects. In the mind's unvisited and sleeping part, it has available both faculties and powers which are not mentioned in the books of historians, in the manuals of mathematicians, or by the psychologists. In this connection Hegel has a meaningful statement: "The sensitive soul oversteps the conditions of time and space; it beholds things remote, things long past and things to come."

Some 1,500 years ago St. Augustine expressed this same insight when he said, "We live beyond the limits of our bodies." Regarding our present situation, in his inspiring book, *The Mysterious Universe*, Sir James Jeans says, "Today there is a wide measure of agreement, which on the physical side of science approaches almost to unanimity, that the stream of knowledge is heading toward a non-mechanical reality; the Universe begins to look more like a great thought than like a great machine. Mind no longer appears as an accidental intruder into the realms of matter; we are beginning to suspect that we ought rather to hail it as the creator and governor of the realm of matter."

In understanding the dimensions of mind there are three aspects of normal consciousness which are of great importance. The first is that the sphere of operation of the conscious mind is extremely limited, that conscious mind is not the whole of a person. It is no more than the apex of a far greater Mind, whose powers and dimensions go beyond our present understanding.

Even the information furnished by the senses is very limited. Through the ear we become aware of vibrations as low as twenty-five per second, through the eye we perceive light (the violet rays) vibrating at over 700 billion cycles per second and through the sense of touch we can feel the infrared heat rays which move too slowly to affect our sense of sight. Certainly we are unable to observe in the physical world what might be evident to living creatures with senses responding to the range of vibrations between what we hear with our ears and what we see with our eyes. It is self-evident that the knowledge of the world which reaches us through our sense organs reveals only an infinitely small part of the living Universe.

We see reality not as it is but as we are. Sir J. Arthur Thomson stated it this way: "The investigator sees nature in the mirror of his mind." In the experience of life each person evolves a mental construct which, by its nature, determines the response of that person to every situation. Everything experienced in life must fit into that structure. You cannot get outside of your own awareness. You dwell within the limits of your own concept. The world and its reality are for you as you see them.

The second fact to observe is that the operation of the conscious mind is intended primarily to secure survival, to enable the individual to make a practical adjustment to his environment.

In the third place, it must be observed that the Universe is not solely composed of those elements which the senses and intellect can reveal and understand but that it extends indefinitely beyond our sensory limits, beyond space and time and beyond the reach of anything that presently can be understood by mind.

In attempting to reach a conclusion regarding the dimensions of mind, it is necessary to remember that only in recent years has limited recognition been extended to the massive data accumulated by research in *extrasensory perception*. The facts revealed in the field of parapsychology and in the area of psychic research are dismissed or discounted by "explanations" which do not account for the admitted facts. Fraud and deception, together with the convenient "unconscious factors," are usually alleged to account for all data not covered by mechanical concepts. The outmoded residual assumptions of eighteenth century scientific thinking still continue, in large measure, to limit our basic ideas regarding the nature and functioning of the human mind.

The facts revealed by parapsychology, when regarded as a whole, establish two important facts. The first fact is that the evidence for the existence of this faculty has been proven beyond any possible doubt. The second is that this faculty does not consist of an extra sense akin to seeing, touching, or hearing, etc. This faculty is not something which makes a direct response to physical stimuli; nor does it operate in the physical world. It is not the kind of thing that can be investigated by the ordinary routine of science.

All the available evidence shows that extrasensory information emerges into consciousness from the subconscious region, an aspect of mind which lies beyond the restricted area of the conscious self in ordinary everyday life.

Extrasensory perception opens a door. It shows that the world revealed by the conscious mind or sensory apparatus is not the whole Universe; and that it is not even complete in itself. These data of mental activity are found to be continuous with an extension of reality lying far beyond the range of our senses.

The origin and source of extrasensory data are probably not in time as we know it—not, that is to say, in the kind of time in which physical processes take place. Extrasensory information about present, past or future events, shows no sign of crossing the kind of boundary which can be separated into past, present and future. This extrasensory information points to the view that the world extends beyond the limits of the conscious mind. It is in this "reach of the mind" pointing to unexplored areas of reality that is found the significance of ESP. These data are of vast importance but the conscious mind tends to reject or ignore these facts because they are unfamiliar and new.

Extrasensory perception covers a wide area of human experience. Just what is the meaning of these premonitions and apparitions, levitations and hauntings, these tales of far sight in time and space, of precognition and retrocognition, of stigmata and faith-cures, of telepathy and hypnosis, of monitions and intuitions like those of Socrates or Joan of Arc? The materials of extrasensory perception are found everywhere in every age and in every literature in every quarter of the globe. That these strange and unusual activities occur is utterly beyond any reasonable doubt. Observed by trained critical minds and found in the experience of many thousands of ordinary people, the question becomes not, what did occur, but what does the occurrence mean? It is in the interpretation that evidence is found for the largely unknown and unrecognized dimensions of mind.

One aspect of extrasensory data is called *telepathy*. During the period around 1850 many competent researchers in England and in Germany investigated the phenomenon of thoughts and messages being transmitted from one mind to another mind at a distance and without any physical force or medium to account for the occurrence. In 1882, after many investigators had come to recognize the possibility of transmitting "thoughts and feelings by means other than the recognized channels of sense," F. W. H. Myers coined the word telepathy to describe these activities. The word means "feeling from far away." Continuing investigations under conditions of rigid control have established the fact that mind is able to communicate with mind without speech or the medium of the familiar sense channels.

In his book, *Man, The Unknown*, Dr. Alexis Carrel, a Nobel Prize Winner in Physiology and Medicine, made the declaration that "Clairvoyance and Telepathy are a primary datum of scientific observation."

Telepathy now appears to be the normal method of communication between the subconscious minds of individuals at a distance from each other. Since these communications are a part of the subconscious process, only in exceptional cases do the messages transmitted emerge into the conscious mind. In this form of communication, distance in space or time seems not to exist. These telepathic phenomena transcend the usual five senses through which the conscious mind sends and receives information. As in other forms of subconscious activity, telepathy usually (but not always) appears when the conscious mind is in abeyance, as in sleep, trance or hypnosis.

No evidence has been found to support the theory that telepathic communication has something to do with "brain-waves" nor is it related, so far as present knowledge is concerned, to electromagnetic waves of the type now understood by the theoretical physicist. Telepathic communication occurs below the threshold of consciousness "by means other than the recognized channels of sense." But the manner in which the communication is sent or received remains a profound mystery.

No purpose would be served by retelling the numerous investigations under controlled conditions that have been made during the last 100 years regarding this phenomenon. That these communications do occur is, as Carrel stated, "a datum of scientific observation."

Those who know of the achievement and critical analytic mind of Luther Burbank will not suspect him of wishful thinking, fantasy or misstatement of facts. In *Hearst Magazine* for May, 1923, Luther Burbank wrote: "I inherited my mother's ability to send and receive communications. So did one of my sisters. In tests before representatives of the University of California she was able, seven times out of ten, to receive messages sent to her telepathically. My mother, who lived to be more than ninety-six years of age, was in poor health the last years of her life. During these years I often wished to summon my sister. On such occasions I never had to write, telephone or telegraph to her. Instead, I sent her messages telepathically, and each time she arrived in Santa Rosa, California, where I lived, on the next train."

Luther Burbank's experience is only one of the many that can be cited as examples of paranormal activity—that is, activity in which "the reach of the mind" is found to extend into an area of cognition not explored or revealed by conscious mind mentation.

One of the best known instances of extrasensory perception or knowledge is that of Edgar Cayce of Virginia Beach, Virginia. With only nine years of ordinary school work, this man demonstrated the mind of a master physician while in a trance-like state. While under trance, Cayce could speak authoritatively on any subject—history, prehistory, geology, electronics, medicine, creation, life after death, even the future. In trance he could speak a score of foreign languages fluently, although when conscious he spoke only

English. This miracle man of Virginia Beach left a 90,000-page library of recorded data. While in trance he gave medical advice or "readings" which benefitted many hundreds of ill persons all over the world.

He was visited by some of the best-known psychologists and physicians of his day. They would investigate for days at a time, observing a number of readings and asking hundreds of questions. They would leave with puzzled faces and questions unanswered. Whatever may be the ultimate explanation of the extrasensory knowledge which Cayce exhibited, he stands today as one example of the dimension of mind as revealed by subconscious activity.

A report appeared in two issues of *This Week* magazine in February, 1961, by Jack Pollack, regarding a unique group of individuals functioning at the University of Utrecht. This group was assembled by Professor W. H. C. Tennheff, an expert on extrasensory perception. His investigations are sponsored by the Dutch government. This university has the only chair of parapsychology in the world.

Interestingly enough, many Dutch people have paranormal powers. Holland was the birthplace of Peter Hurkos, whose extrasensory ability located the stolen Stone of Scone for Scotland Yard. This group of unusual individuals have the ability to operate beyond temporal and spatial limitations at will.

Through their subconscious faculty they can see what is going on anywhere in the world. Some can accurately predict future events.

One interesting member of this group is Gerald Croiset. In a very remarkable case this man was called on the telephone by a seaman; the officer of the ship wanted to know what was wrong with the stranded ship. Croiset, 112 miles away, was able to locate a defect in the engine—it was a very small crack. The difficulty was quickly remedied.

Perhaps one of the most spectacular activities of the members of this group is precognition. A few members, like George Croiset, can correctly describe events still in the future; in one instance Croiset was shown a group of chairs arranged for a meeting to be held some time in the future. His account of the occupant of each

172 THE DIMENSIONS OF MIND

chair proved to be factually correct. His description included facial scars and equally definite personal characteristics. He also indicated which chairs would be vacant.

The most practical factor regarding this group is the fact that these people can, unlike average individuals, demonstrate their ability at will.

Even more important is the overall fact definitely established that men can transcend the limitations of time and space. Innumerable other instances from almost every nation also indicate the existence of a timeless, spaceless dimension of mind.

Emergency situations frequently result in dramatic exhibitions of subconscious power. Consider now one classic instance of persons being *forced* into activity in the higher dimensions of mind through the pressure of a crisis. First Mate Robert Bruce, on a sailing ship out of Liverpool, glanced through the porthole of the captain's cabin and was amazed to see a stranger at the captain's desk, writing on a reckoning slate. Bruce hurried to the captain with a report of what he had witnessed. The captain conducted an immediate investigation.

The stranger, however, had mysteriously disappeared—and had left an equally mysterious message written on the slate—"Steer to the Nor'west." When a complete search of the ship failed to produce the phantom stranger, the captain, much perturbed, changed his course from south to northwest.

A few hours later they came upon a passenger ship, badly damaged and frozen to an iceberg for several weeks. Among the starved and completely exhausted passengers, First Mate Bruce was startled to see the same man who had been in the captain's stateroom. On another slate he was requested to write the words "Steer to the Nor'west," and the handwriting was an exact duplicate of the original message.

The captain of the stranded ship then supplied the information that this man had fallen into a deep sleep at noon, after which he had told of his dream of being on the rescue ship, which he fully described, and had also stated his belief they would be rescued the same day. One puzzling aspect: He did not dream of writing a message on the slate in the captain's stateroom!

Here is an illustration of an important fact. An emergency often actuates what is known as "crisis telepathy" and enables persons to function in areas of mind that seem totally unrelated to the normal processes of consciousness. (Reported by Dr. Robert Galen Chaney of Los Angeles.)

Still another instance is a singular occurrence that points to an area of mental activity, a reach or dimension of mind, which in all its aspects is not associated with or dependent on a normal human brain.

Snow and rain fell in violent fashion on the streets of Philadelphia. It was early December, and as night came the wind rose to blizzard force. Dr. S. Weir Mitchell, America's foremost neurologist during the last quarter of the nineteenth century, had retired early. Sleep was just breaking the last strand of consciousness when his doorbell rang. Dr. Mitchell got out of bed and went to the door. Standing in the snow was a little girl dressed in a cheap thin dress. About her shoulders was a ragged shawl. "My Mother is very sick," she declared. "Won't you come, please?" Dr. Mitchell explained that he had already gone to bed. He told the child that there were many other good doctors nearby. He asked if the girl's family had no regular physician. The girl's only answer was, "Won't you come, please?" Deep in Dr. Mitchell's mind was a memory of the Hippocratic oath. He asked the girl to come inside and proceeded to dress. The girl said nothing more, but when the doctor had put on his heavy coat, she indicated that he was to follow.

They walked several blocks through the snow and rain and entered a house. There the doctor found a woman dangerously ill of pneumonia. The woman had once been a servant in Dr. Mitchell's home. The girl did not follow Dr. Mitchell into the sick room. For a few minutes the doctor was busy examining the woman. When he had finished, he complimented her on the intelligence and persistence of her daughter. The woman appeared bewildered. "But my daughter died a month ago. You will find her clothes in that little cupboard." Opening the cupboard, Dr. Mitchell found the identical dress and shawl which the girl had been wearing. The clothes were warm and dry. They could not have possibly been out in that snow-filled night.

Such is the story of Dr. S. Weir Mitchell, President of the Association of American Physicians, President of the American Neurological Association, holder of degrees from a dozen universities, as he told it on many occasions.

In considering the dimensions of mind, it must be recognized that telepathy makes imperative a revolution in current ideas about the human mind and that precognition demands an equal rethinking of current ideas about time. Just here we should recall the statement of Thomas Hardy as quoted by Dr. Edmund W. Sinnott in his book, *Cell and Psyche:* "We fool ourselves if we imagine that our present ideas about life and evolution are more than a tiny fraction of the truth yet to be discovered in the almost endless years ahead."

The creative dimension of mind is best shown by subconscious mentation. In his *From Unconscious to the Conscious,* the brilliant French investigator, Gustave Geley, a century ago made this statement: "The data of intuition lie beyond facts, experience, and reflection, and surpass them all. Intuition is the very essence of subconsciousness."

As the writer Alice A. Bailey has said: "Intuition is the ability to arrive at knowledge through the activity of some innate sense, apart from the reasoning or logical process. It comes into activity when the resources of the lower mind have been used, explored and exhausted. Then, and only then, the true intuition begins to function. It is the sense of synthesis, the ability to think in wholes, and to touch the world of causes."

It was Albert Einstein himself who said: "The really valuable factor is intuition." Louis Pasteur made this statement: "Intuition is given only to him who has undergone long preparation for receiving it." That this statement is meaningful is evidenced by the experience of noted scientists and inventors throughout the world. Recall the statement of the distinguished research scientist, Dr. Irving Langmuir: "We often underrate the importance of intuition. In almost every scientific problem which I have succeeded in solving, even those that have involved days or months of work, the final solution has come to my mind in a fraction of a second by a process which is not consciously one of reasoning."

Subconscious intuition is the ground from which creative concepts spring. No outstanding inspiration, insight or vision has ever had its origin in the conscious aspect of mind. Our conscious minds provide bread which enables us to survive in the struggle of life, but humanity has never been able to live by bread alone. There are channels of creative energy of which our rational conscious minds know nothing. Perhaps the limitation of those who believe that conscious rational processes are the only channel through which creative insight is received, was stated by Wordsworth in his line, "They peep and botanize on their mother's grave." The basic dimensions of mind are not found in the conscious mind, which may be skilled in adaption but knows little of creative processes. The conscious mind can pluck the petals from a beautiful rose, seeking vainly to probe for beauty in the fast withering spoils. It takes more than rational processes to make a rose.

In our present intellectual atmosphere when one attempts to arrive at a correct concept of the dimensions of mind, it is well to remember the ideal of Thomas Huxley when he said, "Sit down before a fact as a little child, be prepared to give up every preconceived notion, follow humbly wherever and to whatever abysses nature leads, or you shall learn nothing."

In developing a philosophy of man's place and destiny in the Universe, our perspective must be sufficiently broad to include every single known fact. You cannot draw a conclusion about the Universe from the superficial inspection of a six-acre field.

As you develop your own personal philosophy, bear in mind these three basic assumptions regarding the human mind:

1. The Universe in which we live is the result of energy created and directed by mind or consciousness. The ultimate nature of this mind is unknown, except as it may be dimly reflected in the functioning of personality. We can repeat again with Cudworth that "the mind is senior to the world and the architect thereof."

2. Since order, plan and purpose are observed as present in the processes of the Universe, we may assume that self-directing purpose is inherent in the capability of the individual mind. Einstein's dictum that "God does not play dice with humanity" is supported alike by reason and observed facts.

3. The purpose of life exhibiting itself on this planet is to develop by experience the full potential of the individual person. While the full capability of the individual mind is at present unknown, the data reviewed in this study establishes the fact that mind has creative power, that mind is self-directing and also that mind extends out beyond presently recognized limits.

18
YOUR SUBCONSCIOUS POTENTIAL

FREUD, after years of medical practice and the evaluation of this practice by his keen analytical mind, made the decision "to assume the existence of only two basic instincts, Eros and the destructive instinct." In making this assumption, he recognized that human life attains stability and balance only in the presence of two opposing forces. The reality which set the stage for human experience apparently determined that growth, maturity, achievement and peace of mind can only be attained by struggle, by self-directed effort. For self-directed effort to have meaning, there must be the ability to select. The individual mind must have the capability within itself to determine its own course of action, and to move toward a specific goal by volitional choice.

These instincts, or drives, which Freud assumed, are not to be thought of as chemical or predetermined endowments. It is more correct to assume that they are built-in ways of action, or tendencies, necessary for the development of the full potential of human personality.

The concept of Eros, so named for the god of love, is frequently considered in a limited and restricted sense. The instinct for the preservation of the individual and the species is only one aspect of this fundamental creative drive of life. Love, in its all-embracing sense, is the integrative, cohesive and constructing ingredient of human experience. The word love, then, describes more adequately than any other term the creative instinct.

This instinctive love drive is the foundation of all man's creative achievements. His devotion in building a social order of good will and opportunity for all its members; his efforts to express beauty in literature and art; his intellectual and scientific achievements; his insatiable intellectual curiosity which is now thrusting him from his home planet into the depths of space; all these continuing efforts are expressions of this one compelling force—the creative instinct. This instinct is the main stream of the will to live and to develop personality in all its potential.

The destructive, instinctive drive, usually called the "death instinct," is frequently called Thanatos, after the Greek god of death. Its basic purpose seems to be to prevent stagnation and to compel progress and change. Such a condition, or tendency, seems to be necessary if human personality is to attain maturity and continue its evolutionary progress.

In evaluating human experience it is important to recognize that these apparently opposing forces are the necessary ground for all ethical values and for the expression of beauty in art and literature, as well as for the attainment of progress both for the individual and the group. Life does not exist in a vacuum. It is expressed in relationships growing out of the struggle for survival. Without these opposing forces, the only way life could exhibit itself would be a static condition in which movement, organization and change would be impossible.

Someone has said that the lack of enthusiasm is mental anemia. The lack of enthusiasm is expressed in boredom, *ennui* and emotional disintegration. To experience emotion is at least to feel. The crime against life, the worse crime of all, is not to feel the pull and tug of emotional activity. Unfortunately, it seems to be true that there was never perhaps a civilization in which that crime, the crime of torpor, of lethargy, of apathy, and the snake-like sin of coldness-of-the-heart, has been more prevalent than in our technological civilization of the present. This tendency is the modern

painless death, an atrophy of the heart. Without this deeply implanted mechanism, usually described as the struggle for survival,
not only would progress be impossible, but the expression of joy,
happiness, and achievement would be unknown.

There is planted deep in the structure of personality, a mechanism by which these seemingly opposing forces can be directed into
constructive and ego-satisfying channels. It is important to recognize
fully this two-fold nature of mind, and it is equally important to
understand the method by which this two-fold activity of mind is
directed. Let it be repeated again that the conscious mind directs
and controls the subconscious mind. The deeper layer of mind
receives and works upon only that which is given to it by the conscious mind.

A word of caution is in order at this point: The conscious mind
may, and frequently does, misunderstand what the subconscious
mind is attempting to accomplish—the reverse is never true. The
subconscious mind knows completely at all times every tone and
color of that which is in the conscious mind. Its understanding of
the content of the conscious mind is complete and automatic. Many
people fail in their efforts to control the creative aspect of mind
simply because they do not in a single-minded way believe that
the content of the conscious mind determines and controls the expression of subconscious energy. Unless a person with intellectual
integrity actually accepts and acts upon the assumption that the
subconscious is controlled by the volitional aspect of mind, his accomplishments will be limited and in many instances result in
frustration.

It must also be recognized that subconscious mental activity is
present in all relationships and experiences of life. In ordinary business affairs, in professional work and in the simple everyday experiences of home life and personal relations, subconscious activity
whether recognized or not, is always present. Certainly the insight
and wisdom of this part of the mind are not confined to the high
points of creative activity in research, in the arts and in the business world. This part of mind is available and is always present in
every area of human thought or experience

Subconscious mind activity exhibits itself in four stages: As previously emphasized, there must be full and complete *preparation*. All available data must be studied and evaluated. When all the known facts are assembled and fully understood, the problem to be solved, or the objective to be achieved, must be clearly defined and stated as nearly as possible in concrete, cogently described terms. This preparatory phase of subconscious mind-control is of basic importance.

The second phase of this activity is marked by *withdrawal* of conscious attention from the problem and complete relaxation so far as the solution is concerned. This withdrawal from conscious attention to the problem may be accomplished by turning to other work, by engaging in some recreational activity, or simply by dismissing the problem and enjoying natural sleep. Whatever form this withdrawal of attention takes, it must be recognized that there is no orthodox routine or time at which subconscious results arrive in the conscious mind. Perhaps more than at any other time, subconscious insight emerges into the conscious mind immediately after waking from sleep.

The third phase is usually described as the time of *illumination*. It is at this time that the subconscious delivers to the conscious mind its concept of the solution of the problem or its method of attaining the objective desired. Subconscious insight may be complete, or it may simply point the way to the solution. In many instances, especially in situations where full preparation and evaluation of all known facts have been accomplished, the solution to a problem is given in full outline. In instances of this kind, the emerging insight is usually accompanied by an imperative feeling on the part of the individual that the solution is complete and final. More frequently than not, subconscious mentation provides a method, or an approach, to the problem which, when followed through brings the solution. A person should be very careful not to reject a solution offered by his subconscious. The solution given may seem to be bizarre and to violate all rules of reason. The synthesis formed by the subconscious is not limited by conventional logic or by formulae found in textbooks on psychology. It will be helpful to recall Freud's dictum that the subconscious "knows nothing of reason or logic."

The fourth phase of this process is just as important as the three just mentioned. It is the essential function of the conscious mind to sit in *judgment* upon that which emerges from the subconscious. This simply means that the solution offered by the subconscious must be tested and evaluated by the conscious mind. After it is received it must be subjected to cold logic and rational thinking. This, of course, is the function of the conscious aspect of mind.

In evaluating any new insight that arrives from the subconscious, great care should be given to understand the new insight in the perspective of others who have considered the same problem. It is also important that a *feel* for the significance and value of the concept should be fully explored.

Many of the most profound insights of philosophy, science and medicine have been implicit in the thinking of numerous people before someone came along who understood the practical value or meaning of the idea. Modern urban civilization would be utterly impossible without protection against smallpox. Although Edward Jenner is credited, and rightly so, with making this protective measure available, many people previous to Jenner understood the process and actually practiced it. Due to the prevalent resistance to a new idea and the failure to understand its value, this practical measure was never applied to any great extent until Jenner forced it upon the attention of medical authorities and the public.

The same situation prevailed regarding William Harvey's discovery of the circulation of the blood. For hundreds of years previous to Harvey this concept was postulated among isolated thinkers. Harvey finally succeeded in having this idea accepted notwithstanding the virulent opposition of the medical leaders of his day.

In the case of the theory of evolution, Darwin certainly was not the first to entertain this concept. Among many ancient thinkers, the idea of evolutionary development is implicit and in some instances explicit.

Many assume that the atomic structure of matter and the fluid changing nature of energy have been developed only in recent times. These concepts were implicit and, in the case of the atomic structure of matter, explicit in the minds of many Greek thinkers; and these ideas are also found in cultures preceeding the Greek civilization.

Pasteur, whose work and thinking underlies the whole science of modern medicine, was not the first to discover the germ theory of disease. In a similar way, Lister did not originate the idea of antiseptic measures in the presence of wounds. Progress has been delayed and humanity deprived of valuable protective measures for the simple reason that the immediate practical value of these concepts was rejected and delayed.

In directing the subconscious mind, the emotional attitude of the individual is of great significance. If the problem involves a menace to one's status, or to one's employment, or to the health of an individual, fear and anxiety will be present in a greater or lesser degree. At such times the individual experiences frustration and lack of confidence in the process. There is frequently a tendency to blame his condition upon past experiences. In any experience there are two elements—the thing that happens to the individual and the way the individual reacts to that occurrence. Disappointments and threats come into every life and usually cannot be prevented, but the individual can determine his reaction to the situation. Regardless of what occurs to cause the emotion of fear and anxiety, the person activates this fear and anxiety by his own reactions.

It gives the individual confidence and stability to recall the achievements secured by outstanding personalities through subconscious activity. Henry J. Kaiser, who has achieved outstanding success in his industry, states that he owes much of his business success to his habit of using autosuggestion to impress ideas upon his subconscious mind. At one time Henry J. Kaiser had in his employ the young Robert G. Le Tourneau. The creative positive attitude of Kaiser was transferred to the personality of this employee, who   now famous around the world for his manufacture of earth-moving machinery, as well as the inspiration and leader ship which he has given to the religious thinking of millions of people.

An interesting and continuing example of the ability of men and women who are facing problems to redirect their thinking habits and thus solve their problems, is found in the work and ministry of Dr. Norman Vincent Peale, Minister of the Marble Collegiate Church, New York City. Each year hundreds of people ranging over the whole spectrum of our culture, from outstanding business executives to men and women engaged in the ordinary activities of life, come to Dr. Peale for help. In his sermons and his writings, Dr. Peale shares with the public his method of problem-solving and the results achieved.

While each troubled person comes to Dr. Peale with a different problem, his assistance in solving problems can be reduced to a very simple formula. After listening to the problem, Dr. Peale ordinarily quotes some appropriate verse of Scripture which he asks the person to repeat several times a day. This method enables the disturbed person to look away from himself to a source of strength and power which he ordinarily believes to be outside and beyond himself. Since most of these people feel that they themselves cannot solve their problem, this appeal to an Omnipotent Power brings a sense of relief and relaxation. It enables them to escape from what Josiah Royce called "the hell of the inevitable." The repetition of inspiring verses of Scripture implants in the subconscious mind of the individual new hope and expectancy. This enables the individual to turn from a feeling of helpless frustration to one of confidence and a positive mental attitude.

The assumption planted in the subconscious mind of a sustaining strength is accepted by that part of the individual's mind and because of this acceptance, the emotional tone and the outlook of the individual is recreated and new strength is found.

Because these people are usually in a state of anxiety and frustration, this mehtod has the advantage of giving them immediate, expectant hope. Due to the fact that they are experiencing frustration and anxiety, it would be difficult for the average person to

accept the statement that they have within their own mind sufficient power to resolve the problem.

It is quite likely that no man in America has contributed more
to the redirecting and recreating of individual lives than has Dr.
Norman Vincent Peale by his many-faceted ministry.

By the very nature of personality structure, subconscious insight frequently arrives in the conscious mind spontaneously, seemingly without preparation or direction. This statement is inadequate, however; the subconscious can return to the conscious mind
only a synthesis of what has been placed into it. The conscious
mind is usually more effective when it uses the process of inductive reasoning. Since the conscious mind is, of course, limited it
can only consider one thing at a time. On the other hand, the subconscious mind approaches any problem or question by the process
of deductive reasoning. It moves from the general to the particular.

Notwithstanding the fact that subconscious insight occurs spontaneously, it is quite practical to have a planned approach and thus
secure more significant results. This planned approach must be
made by the individual himself. The mind of every individual is
unique and unlike any other mind. There can be, therefore, no
hard and fast outline of steps by which results can be achieved. In
a general way, however, the following suggestions will help to give
order and sequence to any plan for the use of the subconscious
mind by an individual. The plans should be varied so as to fit in
with the individual's other responsibilities, his schedule and his
home life. Since the subconscious mind must, by its very nature,
obey the orders of the conscious mind if plans made to direct the
activity of the creative part of mind are analyzed and stated in
definite terms, results of greater value will follow.

1. It is commonplace to state that every individual should have
an objective, or goal, which he plans to attain. One of the greatest
difficulties for the average individual is to do sustained, realistic
thinking. The majority of individuals can deal with external circumstances much more effectively than they can manage the internal processes of their personality. To do constructive thinking

requires discipline and self-control. Free-wheeling fantasy and day-dreaming, when such processes occur in the absence of a clearly defined objective, are usually an indication of immaturity and may be presymptoms of mental illness. The first step, then, is to visualize a clear picture of your desires, and impress this picture upon the deeper strata of your mind as many times as possible during the day and certainly just previous to going to sleep and the first thing on waking from sleep in the morning.

2. Although modern technology, at least for the great majority of people in this land, has removed the threat of starvation and financial insecurity (in a limited way), at the same time the average citizen experiences a greater degree of stress and anxiety than ever before.

In this situation it is essential that one learns the art of relaxation. This is necessary for the rebuilding of the physiologic processes of the body, as well as for providing a period of creative thinking. The methods for physical and mental relaxation worked out in detail by eminent authorities are available to everyone. In implementing these methods, one must have a feeling of confidence in his own ability and expectant faith that the cosmic process is on his side as a sustaining influence. Such a conception of your ability and of your relationship to Ultimate Reality will do much in helping you to expel from your mental processes negative feelings and self-doubt.

3. There are numerous instances of men and women who are so confident that subconscious insight will be secured that they keep a pencil and pad at their bedside during the night. It is frequently true that impressions rising from the subconscious are tenuous and do not become imbedded clearly in the conscious mind. Unless a record is made at the time these impressions are received, they may be forgotten and certainly are difficult to recall once they are lost.

This method not only applies during the night but during the day when some special thought or "hunch" comes into awareness. A brief record should be made at the time. Even more than during the night, the crowded schedule of activities during the day makes it difficult to regain these momentary flashes of insight, which, in many instances are of supreme importance.

4. Develop an attitude that will give you balance and poise in a changing world. The hard realism of this period has all but extinguished the idealism, glamor and romance of life. The basic concept among the profound thinkers of all ages has been very simple: As we see life, so does life see us. The whole teaching of the *Bhagavad Gita* which has been the inspiration of uncounted millions through many centuries, is that there is but one Reality and that this Reality is to us what we believe it to be. Everything comes from one Substance, or Reality, and our thought qualifies and conditions that Substance and determines what is to take place in our lives.

The fact of our birth is beyond our control. At the end of life, death is inevitable. That we can control and direct our passage between the place of arrival and the port of departure is a fact of unquestioned validity. Of prime importance in this achievement is the use of autosuggestion. If you can believe in the integrity of the processes of your conscious mind, the practice of talking to yourself will be of vast significance in achieving your goal.

5. Make a confidant of yourself but of no one else. The doubts, anxieties and criticisms of others with whom you may discuss your plans will infiltrate your mind and dissipate your strength. In the privacy of your own room, stand before a mirror and state in an attitude of honest emotional sincerity what you expect to achieve. If your situation permits, these affirmations, when you are looking yourself in the face and talking to yourself, should consist of spoken words. While there is no data to prove this statement true except the observed experience of individuals, words do have a power and influence upon the individual that unverbalized thinking does not have. This idea is imbedded in all the great religious traditions of the human family.

6. Finally, trust the impressions, hunches and insights delivered to your conscious mind. Do what your subconscious tells you to do. Perhaps the subconscious illumination will cover only a limited area

of your path but like the small lamps worn on their caps by coal miners, the light given will be sufficient for one step forward, and as you take this step, further light will be available.

In understanding your subconscious potential you must recognize the fact that the conclusions it delivers and the expressions of its creative energy and wisdom are made known through many varied activities. In the ordinary affairs of life, these activities may seem so commonplace that they are seldom observed or recorded. Despite this, there are innumerable instances of subconscious action which are both strange and dramatic. These instances are an indication of the unrecognized and seldom used powers of the subconscious.

During the War Between the States in our nation's capital two incidents occurred—one illustrating the creative power of subconscious processes, and the other apparently indicating that events of the future are known to the subconscious. During the night of November 18, 1861, the city of Washington was shrouded by heavy fog. On this particular evening, long lines of battle-weary soldiers marched past the Willard Hotel. Weary and exhausted they marched with heavy hearts from the defeat of the previous days to the uncertainties of the future.

In a corner room of the Willard Hotel, facing the street, a Boston social leader sat beside the window in her darkened room watching the long line of men going past in the gloom. On an ordinary occasion Julia Ward Howe would have been asleep at this hour. Something within her mind focused her attention upon the yellow rays from the gas light on the opposite corner, which gleamed on the gun barrels and bayonets of the Union soldiers. Mrs. Howe watched the long line of marching soldiers for hours before she decided to retire.

Exhausted from her long train ride from Boston, she slept soundly. Just before daylight she found herself seated at the writing desk in the corner of her hotel room. Writing rapidly, her pen inscribed line after line across the paper, lines that were to make Julia Ward Howe famous. The room was dark and she did not light the candle. Some deep inspiration was being recorded.

It was long after daylight when she left her bed and prepared for the duties of the day. She glanced at the desk and found that she had written a poem of five verses on a sheet of stationery belonging to the government bureau where her husband worked. Mrs. Howe vaguely recalled being at the desk but could remember nothing of what she had written. The manuscript was there, however, and so correctly written that she found it necessary to change only four words in the entire poem. The poem was titled "The Battle Hymn of the Republic" but Julia Ward Howe could recall neither the verse nor the title. She mailed the poem to the *Atlantic Monthly* and it was published in the February issue of 1862. Her compensation was a check for $4.00.

Afterwards Mrs. Howe said of her masterpiece, "I wonder if I really wrote it. I feel that I did not—I was just an instrument; it really wrote itself." Mrs. Howe died in 1910 at the age of ninety-one. A group of 100 children from the Perkins Institute of the Blind furnished the music for her burial . . . "With a Glory in His Bosom that Transfigures You and Me."

The other incident, which suggests that the subconscious mind is capable of precognition, occurred just previous to the death of President Lincoln. The President reported a dream to one of his friends, Ward Hill Lamon, just a few days before he was assassinated. In the dream Lincoln saw a soldier standing over a corpse in the East Room of the White House and asked who was dead—the reply was, "The President—he was killed by an assassin."

The subconscious mind retains what it receives and it functions not only for the great of the earth but also for very humble, limited people. A good illustration of the way the subconscious mind retains everything expressed in its presence is that of a South Carolina Negro man known as the "sleeping preacher" of Lexington County. At that time he was also known as a human graphophone. For several years previous to his death, at varying intervals, this man would preach a sermon during his sleep. The cabin where the sleeping preacher lived had many visitors at night, many of whom heard the man's sermon and appreciated the beauty and strength of the words he used. During these sermons he quoted Scripture texts and references with accuracy and his sermons were delivered in correct English, although the man himself was utterly illiterate.

During his youth this man had been a servant for a well-known preacher who ministered to churches in a rural community. It had been the habit of the servant, whose mentality was never higher than that of a ten- or twelve-year-old person, to place his horse-drawn vehicle outside his master's church and near an open window so that he could listen to the sermon of the day. Like many more intelligent church-goers he soon fell asleep and would remain asleep until the end of the service. The sermons in some unaccountable manner were recorded in the sleeper's mind so that the same words and facts that he had received during sleep many years previous were reproduced with complete fidelity.

We know very little regarding the unrecognized powers of the human mind. Dramatic incidents occurring now and then enable us to see dimly the extended vista of the mind's capability. Because of the limited but significant data available to us, we can join with Flammarion, the French scientist, in his familiar but significant statement: "An invisible world surrounds us; unknown forces are more numerous than known forces; science is merely at its dawn and—let me repeat it—what we know is but a tiny island in the midst of an unexplored ocean."

The mind is a mechanism by which the implanted instincts of Eros and Thanatos are expressed. Not only our conscious minds, but more importantly our subconscious minds, entertain base and dark desires as well as constructive mental and emotional impulses for individual and social progress. The history of art, painting, music, literature and the spiritual growth of the human family is a clear witness to the creative power in the mind of man. The invention of the mind and the altruism men can achieve are awesome to behold. In each of us resides potentials for truth, beauty and goodness beyond imagination. These capacities are an implanted part of man's natural endowment.

Frequently we experience the memory or the intuition that we are banished angels, gods in oblivion. Perhaps we are truly what the old Druids of England believed us to be—Flames out of Heaven.

lit from the fire of God. Though dimmed and limited here with the clay of this physical world, the flame is there, deep in our personality. It may occur someday that the physical environment in which we incarnate will become so transfused because of this flame, so purified, that its light shall shine visible and we shall know ourselves to be gods in embryo—cosmic essences—that were never born and shall never die. When this potential is fully realized in our minds, then we can echo Lord Byron's words: "The Power of thought, the magic of the mind." And we can also affirm with Henley that we have the capability of living a self-directed purposeful life:

> Out of the night that covers me,
> Black as the pit from pole to pole,
> I thank whatever gods may be
> For my unconquerable soul . . .
> It matters not how strait the gate,
> How charged with punishment the scroll,
> I am the master of my fate;
> I am the captain of my soul.